DEVON WI COOKERY BOOK

New and Revised Edition

The Devon
WOMEN'S INSTITUTE COOKERY BOOK

DEVON BOOKS

First published in Great Britain in 1987 by Devon Books

ISBN: 0 86114-797-9

Printed and bound in Great Britain by A. Wheaton & Co. Ltd.

DEVON BOOKS

Official Publisher to Devon County Council
Devon Books is a division of A. Wheaton & Co. Ltd, which represents:

Editorial, Design, Publicity, Production and Manufacturing
A. Wheaton & Co. Ltd.
Hennock Road, Marsh Barton, Exeter, Devon EX2 8RP
Tel: 0392 74121; Telex 42749 (WHEATN G)
(A. Wheaton & Co. Ltd. is a member of the
Pergamon/B.P.C.C. Group of Companies)

Sales and Distribution
Town & Country Books, P.O. Box 31, Newton Abbot, Devon TQ12 5AQ
Tel: 080 47 2690

PREFACE

THE WOMEN'S INSTITUTE IN DEVON

We are friendly, go-ahead, country minded women, who derive enormous pleasure from all the WI has to offer — new friends, fun, companionship, interests, outings and holidays, developing new skills, participating in community services, fighting local campaigns, becoming a WI Markets producer and playing an active role in an organisation which has a national voice.

The WI is the largest women's organisation in the country, and the only one which owns an adult education establishment. At Denman College, you can take a course in anything from car maintenance to paper sculpture, from book-binding to yoga, all levels of cookery to fly-fishing.

There is an Institute near you which meets monthly either in the afternoon or evening. Why not join us? For further information write to the **Devon Federation of Women's Institutes, 56 Heavitree Road, Exeter EX1 2LH,** or telephone **Exeter (0392) 55386.** The minimum age for joining is 16, but we do have junior members who are younger, and there is no maximum age limit. **All** women are welcome.

FOREWORD

It seems scarcely possible that a quarter of a century has elapsed since the Devon WI Cookery Book was first published. It is a measure of the success of the then editor, Mrs Becky Blackmore (then of Peter's Marland WI) that the book has continued to be in demand over that period, and through four editions.

In the last twenty-five years there have been many changes in eating habits and methods of cooking. It has been decided, therefore, that this is an appropriate time to publish a revised edition that will reflect the wide range of skills of our members. Many of the old recipes have been retained, but there are several exciting new ones.

Our thanks are due to everyone who has contributed recipes, and also to the members of the Home Economics Sub-committee, chaired by Mrs Heather Connabeer of Dartington WI, for their work in preparing this revised edition. We wish to record also our thanks to Devon Books for their help and co-operation in the production of this edition.

I feel sure that this book will be of value in many kitchens for another twenty-five years.

Dodo Skennett.

CHAIRMAN
Devon Federation of Women's Institutes

CONTENTS

WEIGHT AND TEMPERATURE CONVERSION CHART

In all recipes in this book the ingredients are shown in imperial measures. However, the metric quantities in this table give approximate conversions calculated to give proportionately correct measurements for successful results.

Dry weight

Approximate gram (g) conversion to nearest round figure	Recom-mended gram (g) conversion to nearest 25g	Imperial ounce (oz)
28	25	1
57	50	2
85	75	3
113	100-125	4(¼lb)
142	150	5
170	175	6
198	200	7
227	225	8(½lb)
255	250	9
284	300	10
311	325	11
340	350	12(¾lb)
368	375	13
396	400	14
425	425	15
453	450	16(1lb)

Liquid measures

Approximate millilitre (ml) conversion to nearest round figure	Recommended millilitre (ml) equivalent	Imperial pint	Imperial fluid ounce (fl oz)
568	575-600	1	20
284	300	½	10
142	150	¼	5

Oven temperature chart

°C	°F	Gas Number	Description
110	225	¼	Very slow
120/130	250	½	Very slow
140	275	1	Slow
150	300	2	Slow
160/170	325	3	Moderate
180	350	4	Moderate
190	375	5	Moderately hot
200	400	6	Moderately hot
220	425	7	Hot
230	450	8	Hot
240	475	9	Very hot

The above oven temperature chart is a guide only and gives recommended equivalent settings, not exact conversions. To be absolutely sure of good results, always refer to your own cooker instruction book.

DEVON SPECIALS

Editor's Note: All these recipes have been sent in as real Devonshire dishes, and only those so marked have been included in this section.

A number of other recipes appearing elsewhere in the book may, we feel, be Devonshire in origin, but were not so labelled by the senders.

1 *APPLE CURRANTY*

2 large cooking apples.
6 ozs. self-raising flour.
A pinch of salt.
1 egg.
4 ozs. shredded suet.
2 ozs. granulated sugar.
2 ozs. currants.
¼ pint milk.

Peel and cut apples into small pieces.
Turn into a basin and mix with suet, flour, sugar, salt and currants.
Stir in egg and enough milk to give dropping consistency.
Grease a 1½ pint-dish and spoon in the mixture.
Bake for 1 hour at 375 deg. F. (190°C) or Regulo 5.
Serve hot with whipped cream.

Appropriate preparation time 20 minutes.
Cooking time 1 hour.
Enough for 6 people.

2 *APPLE-IN-AND-OUT*

½ lb. self-raising flour.
¼ lb. suet.
A pinch of salt.
6 ozs. sugar.
2 large cooking apples.
Milk.

Peel, core and chop apples.
Mix flour, sugar, suet and chopped apples to a fairly stiff consistency with milk.
Bake for 1 hour, No. 5 Gas, 375°F (190°C).
Turn out of dish, sprinkle with sugar and serve with Devonshire cream.

3 *To COOK BEETROOT (Devon Style)*

Wash and peel beetroot—raw.
Slice, or cut into dice.
Place in saucepan and just cover with water; add a little salt.
Simmer until soft (about 20–30 minutes, according to age of beet).
Remove beet from juice with perforated spoon.
To the hot juice add vinegar (about 3 tablespoons) and sugar to taste.
Pour this juice back over the beet and allow to cool.

4 *CUTROUNDS or SPLITS (North Devon)*

- 1½ lbs flour.
- ½ gill milk.
- 4 ozs. butter or margarine.
- 1 oz. lard.
- 1 oz. yeast.
- ½ teaspoon salt.
- ½ teaspoon sugar.
- 1 gill warm water.

Mix yeast with sugar and add the warm water and a tablespoonful of flour.
Leave to rise in a warm place covered with a cloth.
Put milk, butter and lard in a saucepan in a warm place.
Put flour into a warm mixing bowl in a warm place.
Put the milk, etc. and yeast into a well in the middle of the flour, mix into a soft dough and put to rise.
When well risen, knead up into small rounds, put on a greased baking tin and allow to rise again.
Bake in a moderate oven.
When cooked, wipe over while still hot with buttery paper, and cover with a cloth to keep exterior soft.

5 DEVONSHIRE APPLE CAKE

Cream 1½ ozs. sugar and 1½ ozs. margarine.
Add 3 ozs. self-raising flour alternately with 3 good tablespoons apple chopped fairly fine, and put into water to keep the colour. No extra moisture will be needed.
Put in a *well greased* pie-dish.
Sprinkle with sugar and grated nutmeg.
Bake about ½ hour at Gas Mark 5 or 4, 350–375°F (180–190°C).
Can be eaten hot or cold.
This quantity fills a small 7-inch pie-dish.

6 DEVON APPLE FRUIT CAKE

(The Family Fruit Cake)

Beat 4 ozs. margarine in a basin until creamy.
Then add and beat in 4 ozs. sugar.
Dissolve ½ teaspoon baking soda in 1 dessertspoon hot water, mix with ¾ cupful of sieved stewed apple and stir into the fat and sugar.
Add 2 tablespoons of syrup, treacle or honey.
Sift: 6 ozs. flour with a pinch of salt.
½ teaspoonful ground cinnamon.
¼ teaspoon ground cloves.
A good pinch of nutmeg.
Add 2 ozs. picked sultanas, and 2 ozs. raisins stoned and chopped.
Stir the flour and fruit into the wet mixture and mix well together until well blended.
Turn into a greased and papered tin and bake in a fairly slow oven for about 40 minutes.

7 DEVONSHIRE APPLE PUDDING

Mix 1 lb. of stewed and sweetened apples with 4 ozs. breadcrumbs, and put them into a well greased pie-dish.
Top with a sauce made from 3 ozs. butter, 4 ozs. sugar, 3 ozs. ground almonds and a beaten egg.
Bake for ¾ hour to 1 hour in a moderate oven.
Serve hot or cold with blackcurrant jam and whipped cream.

8 DEVONSHIRE BLOCK CAKE

¾ lb. flour
6 ozs. butter.
6 ozs. sifted sugar.
¼ lb. black treacle.
1 lb. currants or sultanas.
¼ lb. candied peel.
3 large eggs or 4 small ones.
½ gill milk.

(The treacle and peel *may* be omitted.)

Work butter to a cream.
Then add treacle and sugar.
Add eggs one by one, beating well.
Add milk which should be just warm.
When this has been well beaten add currants and peel and lastly the flour.
Beat well and bake in a slow oven for 2½ hours.
Makes 3 lbs. cake.

9 DEVONSHIRE CLOTTED CREAM

Put fresh milk into a wide bowl and leave to stand for approximately 12 hours in summer and 24 hours in winter.
Stand the bowl over a pan of water and heat this *very slowly* so that the water never boils.
Leave until the surface of the milk has formed a thick crust.
Stand in a cool place until the next day, then carefully skim this scalded cream from the top of the milk.

10 DEVONSHIRE DUMPLING

½ lb. chuck steak.
¾ lb. plain flour.
½ lb. beef suet.
Potatoes.
Shallots.
Parsley.
Salt.

Make a firm crust of flour and suet chopped very fine, and roll out to size of small dinner plates.
Take a pudding cloth, dip centre in boiling water and wring out very dry.
Place on plate and dust with flour, lay the crust on it and put beef cut up small to within half an inch of rim.
Season to taste and fill up with sliced potatoes and shallots.
Take corners of cloth and draw together very tight and tie.
Place in saucepan of boiling water and keep boiling for 2½ hours.

11 DEVON FRUIT CUP

2 lemons.
2 tablespoons honey.
1 pint cold water.
1 small bottle cider.
1 cupful picked strawberries.
Broken ice.

Place one lemon thinly sliced in a large jug.
Squeeze over the juice of the other, and cover with the water.
Stir well, add honey and cider.
Stand on ice, and just before serving add strawberries and a few pieces of ice.

12 DEVONSHIRE JUNKET

Put some new milk in a china or other basin, or else warm cold milk to the same heat as new.
Add to it a little calf's rennet, and if approved a little brandy or rum may be added also.
Stir with a spoon to mix perfectly.
Place near the fire or on a warm hearth until turned, but it must not be too hot or it will not turn properly.
When turned, put sugar, grated nutmeg, or nutmeg and ground cinnamon, on the top, and scalded or clotted cream, without breaking the curd, and serve.

13 DEVONSHIRE OMELETTE

3 large cooking apples.
½ oz. fresh butter.
2 tablespoons caster sugar.
Powdered cinnamon.
2 tablespoons powdered macaroons.
2 eggs.

Peel, core, and cook the apples in a pan with three tablespoons of water, and the sugar, until it is a soft pulp.
Add the butter and mix thoroughly, also the powdered cinnamon, macaroons and the beaten yolks.
Whisk the whites to a stiff froth and stir lightly to the other ingredients.
Thickly butter a fireproof dish and pour in the mixture.
Dredge the surface with caster sugar, and place the dish in a moderate oven for about 20 minutes until it is puffed up and brown.

14 DEVONSHIRE PUDDING

2 large free-range eggs.
2 ozs. butter.
2 ozs. caster sugar.
2 ozs. plain flour.
½ pint good milk.
Grated rind of 1 lemon.

Cream butter and sugar with lemon rind.
Add eggs beaten well with flour, make a batter with milk added last.
Turn into soufflé dish well floured and buttered, and bake in a medium oven for 30 – 40 minutes.

15 DEVONSHIRE SPLITS

(Ingredients for approximately 14 to 18 splits)

1 lb. plain flour.
½ teaspoon salt.
½ pint skimmed milk.
½ oz. yeast.
1 teaspoon caster sugar.
2 ozs. butter.
Jam.
Devonshire cream.

Grease and flour baking sheets.
Sift flour and salt into a mixing bowl.
Warm the milk to blood heat.
Cream the yeast with the sugar.
Melt the butter in the milk.
Pour all at once into the centre of the flour and mix to a soft dough.
Put into a floured bowl, cover with a damp cloth, and set to rise in a warm place until double in bulk.
''Rub down'' the dough and divide into equal portions (14 to 18).
Knead into small balls with the palm of the hand.
Place on the prepared baking tin.
Prove for 10 – 15 minutes.
Brush with milk and place in a hot oven (425°F, 220°C or Regulo 8) for 15 to 20 minutes.
When cooked brush with a syrupy mixture to make them soft and sticky.
When cold, split and fill with Devonshire cream and jam.

(Note: Syrupy mixture consists of 4 ozs. sugar, one-eighth pint milk. Heat to 215°F, 100°C.)

16 DEVON TROUT AND MUSHROOM PÂTÉ

1½ lbs. of fresh-caught trout (either one large fish or several small).
4 ozs. farm butter.
2 ozs. field mushrooms.
Salt and pepper.
Dash of anchovy sauce.

Clean the trout, but do not remove the heads.
Put knob of butter into the slit stomachs, wrap in greaseproof paper, and steam for ½ hour.
While the fish is cooking, chop the mushrooms (including stalks) very small and fry in butter.
When fish is ready, carefully remove all bones, skin and heads, but retain any liquid, melted butter, etc. from the paper.
Mash the meat with a fork, add the liquid and the fried mushrooms together with any butter left in the pan, add a dash of anchovy sauce and pepper and salt.
Melt remaining butter and mix.
Beat the mixture with a fork until smooth and creamy, then place in

pots (empty meat paste pots are ideal), packing the pâté well down.
Fill nearly to the top, then seal with a small amount of melted butter.
Put in a cool place, preferably a fridge, to set.
When cold cover as jam.

This pâté can also be made with salmon or peel (sea trout).
It is delicious eaten on hot toast, or in sandwiches, or makes an unusual hors d'oeuvre.

17 DEVON CYDER APPLE CAKE

4 oz. soft margarine.
4 oz. caster sugar.
2 large eggs.
4 oz. self-raising flour.
⅜ pint cyder.
1 large Bramley apple.
4 tablespoons brandy.

Decoration

½ pint double cream.
1 – 2 drops vanilla essence.
1 teaspoon caster or icing sugar.
1 red-skinned apple.

Make as Victoria sponge but add grated Bramley apple.
Cook in greased medium sized savarin tin at 180°C (350°F, Gas Mark 4) for 25 to 30 minutes. Cool on a wire rack. When cold put back in savarin tin and soak with the cyder and brandy.
Coat cake with the cream which has been whipped with sugar and essence.
Decorate with slices of red-skinned apple, red side up.

18 DRINKING CAKES

1 lb. plain flour.
3 ozs. butter.
3 ozs. sugar.
2 – 3 ozs. currants.
1 oz. yeast.
A pinch of salt.
Milk to mix.
¼ dram saffron.

Cover saffron with boiling water and leave to steep for several hours.
Mix yeast with a little sugar and cover with a little warm milk.
Set in a warm place to sponge.
Rub butter into flour, add sugar and cleaned fruit.
Warm the milk.

Make a well in the centre of the mixture and put a little warm milk, then add the yeast and saffron.
Add more milk, gradually mixing the flour from the sides of the bowl.
When a fairly dry dough is obtained, take out and knead on a floured board for about 1 minute.
Put in a warm bowl, cover and set to rise in a warm place, for about 1 hour.
Knead again for a minute or two.
Break off pieces of dough and form into large flat cakes.
Put on a flat baking tin, cover, and set to rise again for ½ – ¾ hour.
Bake in fairly hot oven.
When cold split in half and spread with butter.

19 FARMHOUSE GINGERBREAD

Sift together 2½ cups flour, ½ cup cornflour, 2 level teaspoons allspice, 1 level tablespoon ground ginger.
Add ¾ cup brown sugar and ½ cup chopped crystallised ginger.
Melt ½ cup butter or margarine.
Add 8 tablespoons treacle and mix thoroughly together.
Beat 1 egg and mix with ¼ cup milk.
Stir carefully into the dry ingredients.
Dissolve 1½ teaspoons bicarbonate of soda in a little milk and add the mixture.
The batter should be of a thick pouring consistency.
Beat thoroughly before pouring into a greased tin, 7 inches square by 2 inches deep.
Bake for 1¼ hours at Gas 4, 350°F, 180°C.
Serve hot or cold, cut in squares.

20 GRANDMOTHER'S FIGGY JAM

(The Children's Favourite)

3 lbs. rhubarb.
1 lb. raisins.
A little water.
Sugar.

Cut the rhubarb up into short lengths.
Stone and halve the raisins; it is nice to see the raisins in it, but they can be chopped up if preferred.
Cook gently until the raisins' skins are tender before adding the sugar.
Buy the raisins early in the year while you can get those big fat ones we had in the old days for Christmas puddings, and keep them until rhubarb is plentiful enough for jam making.

21 *PARSLEY PIE*

Line a shallow dish with pastry.
Mince or chop up fine some bacon, cover the bottom of dish.
Chop up parsley, enough to cover the meat.
Add pepper and salt to taste.
Beat up 2 eggs and add to the parsley, etc.
Cover with another layer of pastry.

22 *PIGEON PUDDING*

2 pigeons.
About ¾ lb. interlean bacon in strips.
1 tablespoon seasoned flour.
Chopped parsley.
Good pork stock.

For crust:
8 ozs. self-raising flour.
4 ozs. suet.
¼ teaspoon salt.
Water to mix.

Halve the pigeons, and, with the livers, roll in the seasoned flour.
Wrap the bacon around the pigeon halves and livers and put in a basin.
Sprinkle with chopped parsley.
Add sufficient pork stock barely to cover.
Have ready the suet crust, cover the basin with this and tie it down.
Let it boil fairly quickly for 2½ to 3 hours.

23 *PORK PASTIES*

12 ozs. of good short pastry.
About 12 ozs. of cooked pork.
Grated onion.
1 teaspoon Worcester sauce.
Seasoning.

Chop the pork and mix with grated onion, sauce and seasoning. Roll out the pastry thinly and cut into rounds.
Divide the filling equally between the circles.
Fold over the pastry, damping the edges so as to get a good seal.
Flute the edges, brush with milk or beaten egg, and bake in moderate oven for about 20 minutes.

24 POTATO PASTY

Short crust pastry.
New potatoes.
Cream.
Seasoning.

Line a deep plate with short crust pastry.
Fill with scraped sliced new potatoes (raw).
Season well and add some thin cream.
Cover with a pastry top.
Bake in a quick oven at first, then slower to cook potatoes.

Note: Young turnips can be substituted for potatoes.

25 SAFFRON CAKE

1 lb. 2 ozs. flour (plain).
2 ozs. mixed peel (if liked).
8 ozs. currants and sultanas.
3 ozs. sugar.
4 ozs. margarine.
4 ozs. lard.
Saffron.
A pinch of salt.
½ oz. yeast.
Tepid milk.

Sift flour and salt into a warm bowl and rub in fats.
Add fruit and stand in a warm place.
Cream yeast and sugar until liquid, and stir in tepid milk.
Make a well in centre of flour and pour in liquid.
Mix to a soft dough, adding a little more milk if needed.
When dough is smooth, and leaves side of bowl clean, turn on to a lightly floured board and knead for about 5 minutes.
Return to bowl, cover with a damp cloth and leave to rise until it has doubled its bulk.
Remove dough and knead lightly.
Put into warm greased tins and place in a warm place to rise again.
Bake in a moderate oven for 50 – 60 minutes (about 375°F, 190°C).

26 SAVOURY PASTIES

½ lb. damsons.
2 tablespoons water.
½ teaspoon nutmeg.
12 ozs. chopped cooked pork.
1 finely chopped onion.
Seasoning.
8 ozs. plain flour.
2 ozs. margarine.
2 ozs. cooking fat.
Water to mix.
1 beaten egg.

Wash and stone the damsons.
Put fruit into a saucepan with the water and nutmeg, and stew gently until cooked.
Mix the pork with the onion.
Season to taste.
Sift the flour and pinch of salt and rub in the fats.
Mix to a smooth dough with the water.
Turn on to a floured board and cut into 6 circles.
Drain the plums and mix the fruit with the pork.
Put one portion of mixture in centre of each piece of pastry.
Fold pastry in half, dampen edges and seal.
Brush tops of pasties with beaten eggs.
Bake in moderate oven for about 30 minutes.

27 SQUAB PIE

South Devon Variety. For 4 people

4 mutton chops (preferably neck).
4 medium-sized potatoes.
4 medium-sized onions.
2 cooking apples.
Pepper and salt for seasoning.
1 teaspoon granulated sugar.
¾ cup water.
Short crust pastry (not too rich).

Peel the potatoes and onions, peel and core the apples and cut them all into ¼ in. dice.
Trim the chops.
Place a layer of potatoes into a dish of appropriate size.
Add a layer of onions, then one of apples, seasoning as you go with the salt, pepper and sugar.
Add the chops and cover them with the rest of the apples, onions and potatoes, finishing with the potatoes, all well seasoned.

Pour in the water and cover the dish with the pastry.
Cook at 400°F, 200°C (6) for ¾ hour (or until brown).
Then cover with greased paper and cook at 300°F, 150°C (2) for ½ hour.
Serve at once.

28 *TOMATO CHUTNEY*

3 lbs. tomatoes (red or green).
3 lbs. apples, a few cloves if liked.
1 lb. onions.
1 lb. sultanas.
3 lbs. sugar (moist or demerara).
1 teaspoon salt.
2 ozs. mixed spice, or less.
1 quart vinegar.

Peel, core and cut up the apples and onions, simmer all together until well cooked, about 2 hours.

This is a very old recipe handed down in the Devon village blacksmith family at Widecombe-in-the-Moor.

29 *YEAST CAKE*

1 lb. plain flour.
2 ozs. margarine or dripping.
1 egg.
2 ozs. sugar.
A pinch of salt.
½ oz. yeast.
¼ lb. mixed sultanas and currants.
1 oz. lemon peel.
Warm milk.

Rub fat into flour and put to warm.
Put yeast to rise in 3 teaspoons warm water.
Clean fruit and grate lemon peel.
Mix all dry ingredients together.
Mix yeast with warm milk and whisk in egg.
Mix all together into a soft pliable dough and return to bowl.
Allow to rise in a warm place till doubled in size.
Knead into small buns or cakes.
Put into warmed and floured tins and bake in a moderate oven.

SOUPS

30 CONSOMMÉ

Basic Recipe:

- 1 quart first brown stock.
- 4 ozs. lean juicy beef.
- 1 egg white and shell (crushed).
- 1 small onion.
- 1 blade mace.
- 6 white peppercorns.
- 1 piece celery.
- 1 medium carrot.
- 2 teaspoons salt.

Remove all traces of fat from surface of stock.

Shred beef finely and soak in ¼ pint cold water to extract protein.

Put the prepared beef and all the ingredients, including unbeaten egg white and crushed shell, into a large deep pan.

Whisk steadily over gentle heat until boiling point is reached.

Remove whisk and allow the stock to boil up 3 times. Leave the covered pan in a warm place and allow the stock to infuse for about 20 minutes.

If a garnish is to be used it should be cooked now whilst the stock is infusing. Cook garnish in boiling water.

Strain the stock through a dry cloth 3 times. (The egg shell and partially coagulated egg-white act as a filter at this stage).

Reheat the strained liquid *but do not allow to boil,* otherwise the soup will become cloudy.

Put the prepared garnish at the bottom of a hot tureen and pour on to it the consommé.

Garnish à la Julienne. Very finely shredded carrot, turnip, celery (1 tablespoonful of each to 1 quart consommé).

31 CREAM OF WATERCRESS SOUP

- 2 large bunches of watercress.
- 1 quart white stock.
- 1 lb. potatoes.
- 1 oz. butter.
- 1 oz. flour.
- Pepper and salt to taste.

Wash the watercress and leave to dry and then chop finely.
Put the stock into a saucepan with peeled and chopped potatoes, salt and pepper and simmer till tender.
Drain water into a basin and rub the potatoes through a sieve.
Melt the butter and stir in the flour and then add the potato water, stir till smooth and boiling then add potato purèe.
Cover and simmer for 20 minutes, then add watercress.
Cover again and simmer for a further 5 minutes.
Serve with fried croûtons.

32 FRENCH ONION SOUP

For 4 persons

4 medium onions (chopped).
1 oz. butter or margarine.
1 tablespoon flour.
1 cup hot water.
Seasoning.
1 pint milk.
4 small slices hot toast.
2 heaped tablespoons grated cheese.

Fry chopped onions in butter for 5 minutes.
Stir in flour and seasoning and cook for a few minutes.
Gradually work in the hot water, stirring until smooth.
Simmer with lid on for 10 minutes.
Add milk and cook for a further 5 minutes.
Put a slice of toast in each soup plate, pour the soup over.
Add cheese and brown under the grill.

33 LEEK SOUP

6 medium-sized leeks.
3 ozs. margarine.
1 quart milk.
3 large potatoes.
Pepper and salt.

Slice leeks in small pieces and toss in melted margarine in large saucepan.
When thoroughly blended add milk and bring slowly to the boil.
Let simmer for ¼ hour then add potatoes cut in small cubes and simmer all together for 1½ hours, stirring constantly.
Add salt and pepper to taste.
Makes a meal for six people.

34 LENTIL SOUP

8 oz. red lentils.
1 small onion, chopped.
2 tablespoons tomato purée.
1 rasher back bacon, fat removed, and diced.
1 teaspoon thyme or oregano.

Wash lentils thoroughly and leave to soak in cold water overnight (or at least 2 hours). Rinse lentils well, and place in saucepan with bacon, onion and herbs plus 1½ pints of water. Bring to boil and boil for 5 minutes, then simmer until tender. This can be 30–40 minutes, depending on age of lentils.

Sieve or liquidise, if a smoother soup is wanted. Stir in tomato purée and mix well. Serve hot with wholemeal rolls or crispbread. The bacon may be omitted for a vegetarian soup. This soup is extra nice if garnished with crispy bacon – grill streaky bacon until really crisp, then crumble and sprinkle on soup.

35 PEA SOUPER SOUP

½ lb. split green dried peas.
3 pints bacon stock.
1 large onion, chopped.
2 carrots, chopped.
2 sticks celery.
¼ lb. streaky bacon, chopped.
Tablespoon oil.

Boil the peas in bacon stock for half an hour.

Fry onion, carrots, celery and streaky bacon in oil to brown. Add all vegetables and bacon to peas and boil for 40 minutes. Liquidize and season to taste. Serve with chopped parsley and croutons.

36 SPRING SOUP

1½–2 lbs. belly of pork, with rib-bones.
1 tablespoon natural soya sauce.
4 roasted peppercorns.
4 crushed juniper berries.
1 crushed clove of garlic (or some chopped ramson leaves).
2 bunches watercress.
Same quantity of young nettles (optional).
½ lb. of fresh spinach or seakale beet (Swiss chard).
1½ pints good clear stock made from chicken or pork bones.

Cut the rib-bones and rind off the belly pork and cook in the stock with peppercorns, juniper berries and salt to taste, till the meat comes off the bones easily. Lift out bones and rind and discard.

Meanwhile, trim the rest of the pork, removing most of the fat, and cut into thin slices. Marinate this in the soya sauce mixed with garlic or ramson leaves until the stock is ready. Then brown the meat in a non-stick pan to seal and remove excess fat, and add the cooked pork to the soup.

Bring to the boil, and throw in the watercress, nettles and spinach or seakale after they have been carefully washed. Simmer for about 10 minutes and serve hot, with crusty bread or new potatoes.

(After a bad winter, this soup appears to give your system a refreshing tonic effect. After browning with the pork, the garlic taste also becomes extremely mild. As a bonus, the soup is rather low in calories provided the stock is well skimmed and the meat is well browned in its own fat, which is discarded or reserved for other use).

37 TOMATO SOUP

20 oz. can tomato juice.
3 whole cloves.
⅓ pint chicken stock.
Bayleaf.
Pinch mixed herbs.
2¼ oz. can tomato paste.
1 slice onion.
1 level teaspoon salt.
Pinch ground pepper.
Lemon slices to garnish.

Place all the ingredients in a saucepan, except the lemon slices.
Bring to the boil, simmer 5 minutes.
Strain and serve garnished with the lemon slices.

FISH DISHES

38 *BAKED FISH*

As many fillets as required.
A little fat or dripping.
3 or 4 rashers of streaky bacon.
2 or 3 tomatoes.
Pepper and salt.

Wash and drain the fish but do not dry it.
Melt sufficient fat in a pie-dish to well cover the bottom.
When hot dip the fish into the hot fat so that each piece is coated on both sides.
Lay the fish back in the dish with the halved tomatoes at the sides, add pepper and salt and a little sugar on the tomatoes.
Place the bacon rashers on the top and bake in a moderate oven for about 20 to 30 minutes, or until the fish is cooked through and the bacon crisp.
This is very good served with Chinese sweet sour sauce.

39 *FISH FRYING HINT*

For fish frying with bread-crumbs without using eggs.
As an alternative to beaten eggs for coating fish before dusting with bread-crumbs you can use the following:
Mix a little custard powder in cold water, brush over the fish, dip in the bread-crumbs and fry in the usual manner.

40 *FISH BAKE (with fennel)*

4 portions of pollack, or other firm white fish.
1 large bulb of Florence fennel.
16 oz. can of plum tomatoes.
1 teaspoon chopped fresh basil (or ½ teaspoon dried).
Small onion, chopped.

Lightly oil an ovenproof dish and put fish in bottom. Slice fennel fairly thinly and layer over fish. Roughly chop tomatoes and mix with onion and basil. Pour over fish and fennel. Cover dish with lid or aluminium foil. Bake at 150°C (300°F, Gas Mark 2) for 35 minutes.

41 FISHERMAN'S PIE

1 oz. margarine.
1 oz. flour.
½ pint milk.
1 – 2 tablespoons oil.
1 onion, finely chopped
2 ozs. mushrooms, sliced.
1 hardboiled egg, chopped.
8 ozs. cod, cooked and flaked.
Parsley.
Salt and pepper.
¾ lb. creamed potatoes.
1 oz. butter.

Melt margarine, stir in flour to make roux.
Remove from heat, add milk slowly stirring till smooth. Bring to boil, simmer 2 – 3 minutes.
Gently heat oil, lightly fry onions and mushrooms.
Fold in fish, egg, onion and mushroom to the sauce. Add parsley.
Pour into 2 pint casserole, top with creamed potatoes and dot with butter.
Bake 160°C, 325°F, Gas Mark 3, 30 minutes till golden.

42 FILLETS OF SOLE IN CIDER

2 fillets per person.
2 glasses cider.
Chopped parsley.
2 or 3 shallots.
Flour, butter, pepper and salt.

Put the fillets in a fireproof dish, season.
Sprinkle on finely chopped shallots and pour the cider over.
Cook in moderate oven for 15 – 20 minutes till fish is firm.
Remove fish to hot serving dish. Make up sauce using flour, butter and fish liquid.
Add seasoning and chopped parsley and serve poured over fish.

43 GRILLED SCALLOPS WITH COINTREAU

16 large scallops.
16 thin rashers streaky bacon.
Sea salt, black pepper.
1 teaspoon oregano.
Juice of 1 lemon.
2 ozs. butter.
Large measure Cointreau.
8 tablespoons double cream.
1 tablespoon chopped parsley

Turn grill to maximum heat.
Wrap each scallop in bacon and thread onto 4 skewers.
Season with salt and pepper, oregano and lemon juice.
Dab with knobs of butter.
Place on tray and under grill. As bacon cooks, turn and when all bacon cooked the scallops are done.
Place tray with scallops on over low heat, pour on Cointreau and flame it.
Add cream and stir into juices.
Let it bubble to thicken.
Serve the scallops with the sauce strained over them garnished with parsley.

44 MACKEREL WITH GOOSEBERRY SAUCE

Either boil the mackerel in salted water with a little fennel, or grill sprinkled with a little chopped fennel. Serve with sweetened gooseberries made into a thick purée.

45 MAYONNAISE OF BASS

(Luncheon or Supper Dish)

1 large bass.
½ to 1 oz. of butter.
Bunch of herbs (basil, thyme, parsley).

Remove head, trim fins, and gut the bass. Wash.
Place on well buttered baking dish.
Cover with small knobs of butter and put the bunch of herbs inside the fish.
Cover with a buttered greaseproof paper, or wrap in tinfoil.
Bake in a medium oven about 350°F, 180°C, Gas Mark 4, allowing a little over 10 minutes to the pound.
Remove from the oven, take off paper and skin carefully (the skin will come away quite easily) and put the whole fish on a large dish.
When cold cover with a mayonnaise sauce and decorate to taste, surrounding the fish with lettuce, tomatoes, cucumber and a few green leaves of chopped chives.

46 SALMON

Any size from whole fish to steak for one.
Oil or melted butter.
Salt and pepper.

Wipe fish all over with oil and sprinkle with salt and pepper.
Wrap in tinfoil. Place in saucepan with cold water to cover.
Bring slowly to the boil and simmer for five minutes.
Leave in water to cool.

47 SEAFOOD PANCAKES

4 ozs. wheatmeal flour.
1 egg.
Vegetable oil for frying.
1 oz. flour.
4 ozs. peeled shrimps.
1 drop lemon juice.
2 ozs. finely grated cheddar.
Parsley sprigs to garnish.
Salt and freshly ground pepper.
1 pint milk.
1 oz. butter.
6 ozs. salmon or tuna fish.
2 ozs. shelled cockles.
1 teaspoon tomato purée.

Sift wheatmeal flour and salt into a mixing bowl, make well in centre and break in egg.
Gradually add ¼ pint milk, vigorously beating till thick and smooth batter is formed. Pour in ¼ pint milk and beat again until smooth.
Heat a little oil in frying pan and when very hot pour in small amount of batter. Tip pan quickly so batter runs over bottom of pan. Cook until underside is golden brown, then toss or turn and cook other side until golden brown. Fry 8 pancakes and keep warm.
Place butter, flour and remaining milk in saucepan. Heat, stirring continuously until sauce thickens and boils. Add all fish and cook for 3–4 minutes. Add lemon juice, tomato purée, salt, pepper and cheese.
Stuff pancakes with seafood mix and fold or roll up. Cover with foil and bake in oven at 180°C, 350°F, Gas Mark 4, for 20 minutes.
Serve hot, garnished with parsley. Serves 8.

48 SMOKED HADDOCK MOUSSE

1 lb. smoked haddock.
3 hardboiled eggs.
½ pint milk.
1 oz. margarine.
1 oz. flour.
2 tablespoons single cream.
2 tablespoons mayonnaise.
½ oz. gelatine.

Poach haddock in milk till cooked. Remove from milk and flake into small pieces.
Keep milk.
Flake in the hardboiled eggs.
Make white sauce using the fish milk, margarine and flour. Allow to cool.
Dissolve the gelatine in a little water, add to white sauce.
Add in the fish and eggs, mayonnaise and cream. Blend well.
Put in mould or deep dish to set in fridge.
Turn out when cold and set, decorate to serve. Freezes well.

49 SMOKED SALMON PARCELS

8 ozs. prawns.
3 tablespoons mayonnaise.
3 tablespoons plain yoghurt or sour cream.
A little creamed horseradish sauce or chopped fresh dill.
12 ozs. sliced salmon.
Thin strips of leek or spring onion to tie parcels.
Watercress and lemon wedges.
Brown bread and butter.
Salt and pepper.

Reserve 6 large prawns for garnish.
Put remainder in bowl, add mayonnaise, s/cream or yoghurt, horseradish or dill.
Separate smoked salmon into 12 strips.
Put portion of prawn mixture in centre of 6 strips. Wrap up and use the other 6 to fold the other way to make parcel.
Tie up with either the leek or spring onion strips.
Serve on watercress bed with lemon wedges and brown bread and butter.

50 STEAMED FISH PUDDING

¾ lb. fillets of white fish.
1 egg yolk.
1 lb. potatoes.
½ pint picked shrimps.
1 tablespoon butter.
3 ozs. cheese.
2 teaspoons chopped parsley.
Pepper and salt to taste.

Butter a plain mould thickly and line it with some of the fish fillets.
Boil and mash the potatoes, adding the grated cheese, butter, and beaten egg yolk.
Season to taste with chopped parsley, pepper and salt.
Fill the lined mould alternately with layers of potato purée and shrimps.
Fold remaining fillets of fish over the top.
Cover with buttered paper and steam for ½ hour.
Turn out and serve with shrimp or parsley sauce.

51 TROUT IN NEWSPAPER

1 trout per person.
2 sheets of newspaper per fish.
Bouquet of fresh herbs per fish.
Thin slice of lemon per fish.

Stuff fish with herbs and lemon.
Wrap envelope of paper round each fish.
Run under cold tap until sodden.
Bake at 200°C, 350°F, Gas Mark 4 until paper completely dry. 8 minutes approximately.
Using scissors open package, peel off paper which will lift off skin.
Serve with yoghurt sauce:

½ pint natural yoghurt.
1 tablespoon chopped chives.
Juice ½ lemon.
Salt and pepper.
3 tablespoons peeled and chopped cucumber.
½ teaspoon mint sauce concentrate.

Mix together and chill.

MEAT DISHES

52 BACON FRITTERS

2 rashers bacon.
2 ozs. flour.
½ teaspoon baking powder.
Salt and pepper.
Approximately ½ gill milk and water.

Rind and dice the bacon and fry it till golden brown and crisp.
Then remove it, leaving the fat in the pan.
Mix together the flour, baking powder, salt and pepper, and mix to the consistency of thick cream with milk and water.
Add the diced cooked bacon and place in spoonfuls in the hot fat.
Fry till golden brown on both sides.
Serve at once.

53 BACON JOINT IN DEVON CIDER

2 to 3 lbs. collar.
½ pint rough cider (draught).
6 cloves.
2 ozs. demerara sugar, mixed with 1 oz. fine brown breadcrumbs.

Cooking time 25 minutes to lb., and 25 minutes extra.
Soak the collar for a few hours.
Drain and cook in cider with cloves for ½ cooking time.
Remove skin and sprinkle the fat with sugar and crumbs.
Bake 200°C., 400°F., Gas Mark 6 for remainder of time.

54 BACON AND PINEAPPLE

Have gammon or similar rasher cut 1 inch thick.
Simmer for ¾ hour.
Lift and remove skin.
Lay in a shallow baking or pyrex dish and sprinkle with 1 tablespoon demerara sugar and lay pineapple (rings or bars), 1 or 2 per person, on top.
Brown lightly under grill.
Cover with foil and place in slow oven for about ¾ hour.

55 BEEF LOAF

1 pound lean minced beef.
1 cup bread-crumbs.
1 cup milk.
1 egg.
Salt and pepper.
3 tablespoons melted dripping.
1 tablespoon finely chopped parsley.
1 tablespoon finely chopped onion.

Mix beef, bread-crumbs, salt and pepper and fat.
Add milk which has been combined with egg.
Add onion and parsley and mix all together well.
Pack into a well-greased 1 lb. loaf pan and bake and baste for 45 minutes in moderate oven.

Serves 6 people.
Delicious cold as well.

56 BEEF ROLL

2 lbs. tender beef.
½ lb. lean ham.
½ lb. bread-crumbs.
3 eggs.
½ teaspoon pepper.
1 teaspoon salt.
A little nutmeg.

Put beef and ham through mincing machine, then mix in other ingredients.
Beat in eggs and bind together.
Tie in a damped and well-floured cloth and boil for 3½ hours.
When cold glaze and serve cold.

57 BIBOTY

Mince some cold meat fine.
Cut an onion in fine slices.
Put it into a saucepan with a piece of butter and fry it brown.
Then put in the meat and some curry powder and mix well together

with some milk in a saucepan so that it does not get dry.
Let it simmer a few minutes over the fire.
Then beat up 2 eggs, put the meat in a pie-dish and pour the eggs over without stirring it.
Bake about ½ hour in a slow oven.

58 *BINDALOO*

(A Portuguese Curry)

1 lb. stewing steak cut in squares.
1 dessertspoon curry powder.
1 teaspoon salt.
5 cloves of garlic, medium size. (Peel them and place under blade of knife till they crack and then chop finely.)
2 ozs. margarine (chopped in bits).
½ cup of vinegar.

Wash the meat and when wet add salt and curry powder and mix well.
Add garlic, margarine and vinegar.
Turn well in a china basin or enamel pan (without a chip) with a spoon and leave soaking overnight.
Next day stir round then simmer gently for an hour or so until cooked.

59 *BRAWN*

½ a pig's head.
2 onions.
3 carrots.
2 small leeks.
A few black peppers.
A stick of celery.
Orange and lemon rind.
Bay leaves.
A garlic clove.
A pinch of cinnamon.
½ bottle of white wine.
1 tablespoon of wine vinegar.
4 hardboiled eggs.
Lemon juice.

Wash the pig's head, remove the teeth, singe off any bristles attaching to the skin, and scrape the tongue.
Put it in the largest saucepan you have, add the vegetables, seasoning, wine, vinegar and water to cover.
Simmer the head very gently for at least 3 hours, when all the flesh should leave the bones.
Strain the juice and vegetables through a sieve, remove the fat and return the liquid to the saucepan.
Reduce it by boiling down to half the quantity.
Meanwhile, remove the meat and fat from the bone and skin the tongue.
Put all meat and some fat on a chopping board and chop or slice fairly small.
Taste the stock, which should be dark in colour, and add seasoning if necessary.
Squeeze in the juice of the lemon.
Grease a mould and line it with slices of hardboiled egg.
Put the chopped meat into the mould and cover it with the liquid.
Put a weighted flat plate on top and leave to set.
Serve with rye bread and sliced beetroot soaked in burgundy to which a little sugar has been added.

60 DEVON BEEF CASSEROLE

1½ lbs. chuck steak, trimmed and cubed.
1 tin tomatoes.
½ pint apple juice.
1 medium onion.
1 teaspoon dried herbs.
1 tablespoon rolled oats.
A little oil.

Fry cubed beef in a little oil to seal it. Transfer it to casserole.
Fry onions gently.
Add the apple juice and tomatoes to the frying pan and stir well.
Add the oats and the herbs. Basil is best but thyme, oregano or mixed herbs will do.
Bring just to the boil and pour over the meat.
Cook at 180°C., 350°F., Gas Mark 4 for 1½ hours. Longer will not harm it.
If using a slow cooker cook one hour on high and two on low.

61 CASSEROLE OF RUMP STEAK

Take thick (about 1 inch) slices of rump steak, each weighing about 4–5 ozs.
Fry them slightly in butter or margarine, together with some sliced onion.
When ready place a layer of onions in the bottom of a casserole, then put in the meat and cover it with a layer of cooked onions.
Add to this seasoning, a half pint of beer (for about 2 lbs. of steak), bay leaf (if liked), some thyme, and gravy to cover.
Cook slowly 170°C., 325°F., Gas Mark 3 for about 2 hours.

62 CHICKEN IN CASSEROLE

1 boiling fowl.
1 cup Patna rice.
1 or 2 carrots, sliced or cut in 'matches.'
3 or 4 rashers of bacon.
Pepper and salt.
About 1 quart chicken stock or water.
A blade of mace.

Place the fowl in a large casserole, or double roasting dish.
Put the bacon rashers over the breast.
Arrange the rice, carrots and seasoning round the bird and add the stock.
Place in quick oven for ½ hour, then decrease heat (if using an "Aga" the top oven to start, then the bottom one) for about 1½ hours—2 hours in all, longer for very old bird.
When cooked serve the rice and carrots separately from the fowl.
Any rice which remains will set in a bowl and can be turned out and eaten cold with cold chicken or salad.

63 BARBECUED CHICKEN WINGS, DRUMSTICKS OR THIGHS

Make the marinade, mixing the following in a large bowl:

Half cup dry cider.
2 tablespoon soya sauce.
1 tablespoon honey or thick syrup.
1 tablespoon tomato purée.
1 teaspoon allspice.
1 clove garlic, mashed.
1 level teaspoon salt.
Half teaspoon freshly ground pepper.
1 tablespoon ground coriander.
2 teaspoons mild paprika (for colour).

Prepare the chicken joints and soak in this marinade for two to four hours.
Lift chicken out to drain, and blend a tablespoon of cornflour in the marinade and cook in a pan until a thick red sauce results.
Place chicken joints in this sauce to coat, then place them on a rack to grill or barbeque until they are cooked.
Brush the joints occasionally with this thick sauce, and serve the chicken with sauce as a dip.
Add a teaspoon of chilli powder or cayenne for a piquant sauce if desired.

64 CHICKEN LOAF

13 ozs. diced cooked chicken.
13 ozs. chopped gammon or bacon.
6 ozs. mushrooms.
8 tablespoons chopped parsley.
2 large onions, chopped.
Clove of garlic, crushed.
6 ozs. fresh wholemeal breadcrumbs.
1 large egg, beaten.
4 ozs. Shape cheese, cubed.
Salt and black pepper.

Mix together chicken, bacon, mushrooms, parsley, onion, garlic, breadcrumbs, egg and salt and pepper.
Spoon half the mixture into a loaf tin, press down firmly.
Put cubed cheese down middle of mixture and cover with remainder.
Press down well. Cover with foil, bake one hour at approx. 180°C., 350°F., Gas Mark 4.
Serve in slices hot or cold with salad or rice or on its own as a snack.

65 CHINESE CHOPS

6 lamb chops.
2 tablespoons seasoned flour.
1 oz. dripping.
2 tablespoons Worcester sauce.
1–2 tablespoons lemon juice.
5 tablespoons pineapple juice.
6 slices tinned pineapple.
1 oz. flour.
1 oz. butter.

Trim chops and coat with seasoned flour.
Fry quickly in dripping till each side is golden brown.
Place in a 2 pint casserole.
Heat together Worcester sauce, lemon juice and pineapple juice and pour over chops.
Cover with a lid and cook for 30 minutes.
Remove chops and keep hot on a dish.
Thicken liquid in which chops were cooked with a teaspoon of flour blended with water and pour over chops.
Coat pineapple slices with flour and fry in butter and use to garnish the chops.

66 CURRY BALLS

8 ozs. minced cold meat, raw or cooked.
6 ozs. boiled rice.
Curry powder.
Squeeze of lemon juice.
1 egg.
Bread-crumbs.

Flavour meat and rice with curry powder and lemon juice.
Bind with egg and firm into balls.
Dip in egg then in bread-crumbs.
Fry in little fat or oil a golden brown.
Serve with rice, a curry sauce and chutney.

67 FAGGOTS

Cut up finely ¼ lb. liver, ¼ lb. fat bacon and 2 lbs. onions.
Cook the bacon and onions together in a saucepan for 5 minutes, then add the liver and ½ pint water.
Simmer for 15 minutes.
Add 3 cupfuls of soaked bread-crumbs.
Season to taste with sage, salt and pepper, and mix thoroughly.
Put into a well greased baking tin, cut into squares, brushing over each square with fat, and bake in a moderate oven for ¾ hour.

68 HAM AND CHICKEN FRICASSEE

6 to 8 ozs. ham or bacon.
1 small tin chicken soup.
A little milk.
Bay leaf.
Onion.
1 oz. flour.
¾ oz. butter.
Salt and pepper.
Cooked rice.

Melt butter, add flour.
Make the soup up to ½ pint with milk and add to cooked flour and butter.
Add bay leaf and onion, etc.
Cook for a few minutes, then add diced meat and heat up.
Remove bay and onion.
Pour on dish with cooked rice around and serve hot.

69 ITALIAN SPAGHETTI

2 tablespoons fat.
3 onions.
1 lb. ground beef.
1 tin tomato soup (condensed).
1 tin canned tomatoes.
½ tablespoon chilli powder.
½ tablespoon cinnamon.
Salt and pepper.
Chopped stuffed broken olives.
Boiled spaghetti.

Fry onion and meat in fat till browned.
Add to saucepan of meat the soup, tomatoes, chilli powder, cinnamon, salt and pepper.
Simmer (covered) for 1½ hours.
Add chopped olives before serving.

70 LIVER AND BACON HOTPOT

1 lb. ox liver.
2 to 3 ozs. bacon.
½ lb. onions.
3 lbs. potatoes.
A little dripping.
Salt and pepper.

Wash and slice liver.
Put in a pie-dish or hot-pot jar with layers of sliced bacon and potatoes; season each layer.
Cover with remainder of potatoes and put dripping on top.
Half fill dish with water.
Bake in a moderate oven 1½ to 2 hours.
Three or four tomatoes may be added, cut in slices.
½ lb. cooked haricot or butter beans may be used; these give extra nourishment and make the dish go further.

71 LIVER PÂTÉ

Place in a stone jar:

1 lb. lamb's liver.
1 teaspoon black pepper.
1 teaspoon ground nutmeg.
1 teaspoon ground mace.
1 teaspoon cayenne pepper.
1 dessertspoon salt.
4 ozs. butter.

Cover with lid and stand in saucepan of water.
Cook 3 – 4 hours.
While still hot, put through mincer twice.
Allow to cool before serving.

72 MADRAS CURRY

For each person:

1 oz. dripping.
1 onion.
1 teaspoon curry powder.
¼ pint stock.
Cooked meat.
1 apple, prepared, and } chop small or
1 dessertspoon sultanas. } mince.

Melt fat in saucepan.
Add chopped onion and stir till melted (about 10 minutes).
Stir in curry powder.
Add stock slowly and bring to boil.
Add other ingredients and simmer for about 20 minutes.

Serve with fresh chutneys to taste, e.g.:

Tomato sliced and sprinkled with parsley.
Mint and butter balls.
Sliced banana.
Mango or other sweet bottled chutney.
Bombay duck.

73 MOCK VENISON

Get a small loin of lamb, bone it carefully, mix together a little brown sugar and black pepper, rub it into the part from which the bones were cut.

Moisten with a very little port wine, and leave for a day.

Make a paste of flour and water, roll the loin into a neat shape, cover with paste, put thick buttered greaseproof paper outside this, and bake in a quick oven for about 2 hours.

74 NOISETTE DE VEAU VALENTINO

1½ – 2 lbs. loin of veal, or thin slices from the leg.
2½ ozs. butter.
¼ oz. flour.
¼ pint veal stock.
¼ pint single cream.
2 ozs. mushrooms, sliced.
About a dozen or more asparagus tips.
Lemon juice.
Mousseline potatoes.

Bone the loin and cut the meat in thin slices lengthways.

Bat out and flatten.

Melt 1½ ozs. butter in a frying pan, cook the noisettes in this, then keep warm between two plates.

Dust flour into pan, add stock and cream, bring to boil and season well.

Cook mushrooms quickly in a nut of butter, add a squeeze of lemon juice; add remaining to sauce off the fire and stir in the mushrooms with the asparagus tips.

Have ready the potatoes, arrange down dish, lay veal on top and coat with the mushrooms, asparagus and sauce.

75 HERBY MEAT BALLS

1 lb. minced pork, from shoulder or hand.
½ lb. grated carrot.
1 large Bramley apple, grated and combined immediately with pork and carrot.
2 tablespoons oats or oatmeal.
A good bunch fresh coriander leaves, finely chopped.
A generous pinch of ground coriander.
A few sprigs fresh marjoram or oregano, chopped.
1 large egg, beaten.

Combine all the above ingredients with about a teaspoon of salt and a generous milling of pepper (or season to taste). When well mixed, leave for five minutes for oatmeal to swell slightly and absorb excess liquid.

Meanwhile, heat a pan of vegetable oil to deep-fry the meat-balls, and when hot, drop in a tiny slice of ginger to flavour it. This can be discarded later.

Quickly shape the meat into walnut-sized patties and lower gently into the vegetable oil to deep-fry till golden brown.

Drain on kitchen paper and serve hot on their own as an hors-d'oeuvre or served with cocktail sticks for a party snack. Also good for dinner time with a sauce – Italian-type tomato sauce, Chinese-type sweet-sour sauce or a rich parsley sauce – and served with pasta, rice or sautéed potatoes and onions.

76 NEPTUNE'S NUGGETS

8 ozs. fresh crabmeat.
8 ozs. lean minced pork.
1 grated carrot.
1 grated apple.
1 grated parsnip or turnip.
2 pints of chicken stock.
1 tablespoon cornflour.
1 teaspoon grated horse-radish.
1 teaspoon salt, pepper to taste.
1 teaspoon ground turmeric.
1 egg, beaten.

Bring two pints of good, clear chicken stock to the boil, and keep simmering.

Combine all ingredients and shape into small balls, not more than 1½ inches in diameter, and lower them gently into the stock to poach. The balls will rise to the surface when cooked. Remove and keep warm.

When all nuggets are cooked, shred some green vegetables, cook in the stock, then thicken and serve with the nuggets.

77 PORK AND APPLE CASSEROLE

6 medium-sized apples.
⅓ cup of water.
2 cups of cooked diced pork.
¾ teaspoon salt.
⅓ cup of brown sugar.
¾ cup of moist bread-crumbs.

Peel, core and slice the apples.
Add the water and cook, covered, with the sugar, until soft.
Place half of pork in bottom of casserole, sprinkle with salt and add half the apple sauce.
Repeat, using the remaining ingredients.
Top with bread-crumbs and bake in moderate oven for about ½ hour.

78 PORK IN BATTER

(For an "End of Joint" Dish)

Make a batter as for Yorkshire pudding.
Add a little chopped onion and chopped sage.
Pour into baking dish, in which fat is sizzlingly hot.
Put in pork, cut into chunks, and bake for about 20–30 minutes.

79 POTATO HASH

2 lbs. potatoes.
½ lb. carrots.
1 small turnip.
¾ lb. hashed meat.
2/3 drops of gravy browning.
2 pints water.

Peel potatoes and cut into quarters.
Scrape carrots and dice into about 1 inch squares.
Same with the turnip.
Dice meat into about 1 inch squares.
Put all into a pan, add water, and cook till all vegetables are soft.
Add gravy browning.
Serve hot.
Enough for 6 people.

80 QUICHE LORRAINE WITH HAM

1 cup coarsely chopped leftover ham (boiled or baked).
¼ lb. grated cheese.
1 9-inch unbaked pastry shell.
2 eggs.
1 tablespoon flour.
1 cup milk.
Dash of nutmeg.
½ teaspoon salt.
⅛ teaspoon white pepper.
1 tablespoon melted butter.

Sprinkle the ham and then the cheese into the pastry shell.
Beat the eggs slightly then stir in the flour (I mix this with a little of the milk first) and seasonings.
Pour custard mixture over ham and cheese, and top with the melted butter.
Bake in medium hot oven 375°F., 190°C., Gas Mark 5 for 35 minutes, or until well puffed up and golden brown on top.
Let stand for 5 minutes before cutting.
This quiche may also be served at room temperature.
Makes 4 or 6 servings.

81 SKINLESS GROAT PUDDINGS

½ a pig's head or a knuckle of pork.
2 lbs. approximately, groats.
Seasoning.

Clean and scald joint, then place in a saucepan with water only half covering the joint, and simmer for about 2½ – 3 hours, until tender.
Remove meat from the bones and put through the mincer.
Weigh meat and use equal weight (or less if preferred) of groats.
Strain liquid in which the meat was cooked and in this cook the groats slowly for about 20 – 30 minutes, until tender and the liquid is absorbed, keeping the mixture well stirred.
Mix thoroughly with the minced meat and season to taste.
Place into pudding basins or pyrex dishes and allow to cool and set overnight.
Turn out and cut into 1 inch thick slices and fry in very little fat.
Serve with fried tomatoes and/or bacon for breakfast or supper. Half a pig's head and 2 lbs. groats will make about 3 large basinsful, giving several slices of pudding.

82 SQUAB PIE

2 lbs. neck of mutton.
2 lbs. apples, sliced.
1 lb. onions, sliced.
Suet paste.
1 tablespoon mushroom ketchup.
Sugar, salt and pepper.

Divide the neck into cutlets.
Place them in a pie-dish and season rather well with salt and pepper.
Add the apples and onions in layers.
Sprinkle with sugar.
Half fill the dish with boiling water and then cover with a layer of suet paste.
Bake in the oven for about 1½ hours.
Before serving pour the gravy out at the side, skim off all fat, add the mushroom ketchup, season to taste and return to the pie.
Serve very hot.
Time: About 2 hours. Sufficient for 5 or 6 people.

83 STUFFED STEAMED STEAK

For 4 people get a pound of skirt or stewing steak.
Spread on a board and cover with parsley and thyme stuffing.
Roll up and secure with string and put in a basin.
Cover with greaseproof paper and a pudding cloth.
Steam very slowly for 3–4 hours.
The meat becomes beautifully tender and the gravy is delicious.
Serve with potatoes and any green vegetable in season.

84 TENDER STEAK

(Swiss Recipe)

Thin slices of stewing steak, 3–4 ozs. per head (in pieces about size of palm).
1 onion.
Peas if desired.
2–3 tomatoes.
NO water or stock.

Melt a very little fat in a saucepan.
Put in the chopped onion and place on medium heat.
Sprinkle meat with seasoned flour and place over onion.

Add tomatoes, skinned and cut in thick slices.
Cover closely and after about 5 minutes reduce heat to very, very gentle.
Cook for at least 2 hours, and if you wish to go out, the dish can safely be left for 3 to 4 hours.
A packet of frozen peas may be added at the beginning, or drained canned peas about 20 minutes before serving.
When ready, lift the meat with a strainer on to a fireproof serving dish; brown, if desired, under a hot grill, and pour over it the gravy which will have formed in the cooking process.
Garnish with the vegetables.

85 VEAL AND HAM MOULD

¾ lb. veal.
2 knuckle ends (1 smoked, 1 plain).
A little chopped parsley.
½ oz. gelatine.
1 blade mace.
1 onion.
2 hard-boiled eggs.

Cook veal in water with mace and onion till tender.
Cut into small pieces.
Boil knuckles till tender and cut up also.
Dissolve gelatine in small quantity of stock.
Wet a mould and put a little gelatine in and around sides.
Cut eggs and decorate bottom of mould with them and parsley.
Set with a little more jelly.
Fill in the mould with veal and ham and gelatine stock.
Leave to set.
Turn out and serve.

86 WET ROAST

(Lancashire, 1950)

Take a piece of brisket of beef about 4 lbs. in weight, score the top (as the rind of pork).
Put into a large earthenware casserole 2 onions finely chopped and ½ a thinly-sliced carrot.
Add a little water and seasoning.
Place the brisket on top, cover closely and cook slowly for about 3 hours.
This has to be tasted to be believed.

SAVOURY SNACKS AND SUPPER DISHES

87 BROCCOLI AND BUTTERED EGGS

Broccoli.
Buttered toast.
6 eggs, beaten.
½ lb. butter.

Keep a nice piece for the centre, and have 8 pieces of broccoli to go round.
Boil the broccoli.
Have eggs ready.
Put butter into a saucepan, stir it over heat, add eggs and stir till the mixture is thick enough.
Season, pour over the hot toast and arrange broccoli as directed.

88 CHEESE SCOTCH EGGS

4 hard-boiled eggs.
1 level teaspoon salt.
Pinch cayenne pepper.
1½ ozs. flour.
1 teaspoon Worcester sauce.
1 egg.
6 ozs. grated cheese.
Dried bread-crumbs.
A little milk if necessary.

Mix the cheese, flour and seasonings.
Add beaten egg and mix well.
Using wet hands, coat the hard-boiled eggs completely with the mixture.
Roll them in dried bread-crumbs.
Fry in hot deep fat to a golden brown.

89 CHEESE TURNOVER

2 ozs. cheese.
1 oz. margarine.
1 egg.
Salt and pepper.
4 ozs. pastry.

Melt butter in a saucepan and add grated cheese, and the egg, beaten with seasoning.
Stir over a small flame until the mixture thickens, and set aside to cool.
Roll out pastry quite thinly, cut into rounds or put in tin.
Fill with mixture.
Wet edges and press together.
Bake 15 minutes at 220°C., 425°F., Gas Mark 7.

90 HOT POTATO SAVOURIES

4 ozs. self-raising flour.
2 ozs. margarine or butter.
2 medium-sized cold boiled potatoes.
Pepper and salt.
A little milk.
2 slices green streaky bacon.

Rub margarine into flour, then rub in the potatoes until the mixture is of a crumbly texture.
Add pinch of salt and pepper to taste and ½ small teaspoon baking powder.
Mix by hand lightly until it is like a dough substance.
Form into circular cakes about 2½ inches in diameter and ½ inch thick.
Cover each cake with a strip of green bacon.
Bake in a moderate oven (Regulo 7) for 20 to 30 minutes, until lightly browned.
Serve hot for tea.

91 LEEK PIE

Take 2 lbs. of leeks, clean and cut them into ½ inch lengths, and boil until tender.
Strain and put into a pie-dish, adding 2 ozs. of streaky bacon, cut finely, 2 eggs, well beaten, pepper and salt to taste.
Cover with a good pastry and bake in the oven for ¾ hour.
Sufficient for 4 persons.

92 LETSHO
(Hungarian Savoury)

1 onion.
2 green peppers.
4 tomatoes.
4 eggs.
Salt.
1 cup uncooked rice.
2 tablespoons lard or bacon fat.
1 teaspoon paprika.

In a saucepan heat the fat, fry chopped onion until golden brown.
Sprinkle in paprika and rice and fry 4 minutes.
Add diced peppers, tomatoes and small cup of water, salt.
Cover, and cook for 10 minutes.
Beat up eggs, pour into saucepan, stir till it sets.
Serve at once.
Enough for 4 people.

93 MACARONI BAKE

1 onion, finely chopped.
1 lb. minced beef.
1 can tomatoes.
1 tablespoon tomato purée.
1 teaspoon dried basil.
Salt and pepper.
3–4 ozs. wholewheat macaroni.
Butter.
Plain flour.
½ pint milk.
Cheddar cheese.
English mustard.
1 oz. grated cheese.
1–2 ozs. dried breadcrumbs. (or finely crushed crisps).

Gently fry onion, add minced beef until brown.
Stir in tomatoes, tomato purée, basil and salt and pepper. Simmer 15 minutes.
Cook macaroni for 15 minutes, drain, add to meat. Turn into casserole dish.
Make cheese sauce, pour over meat and macaroni.
Mix together topping ingredients, sprinkle over cheese sauce.
Bake uncovered for 30 minutes at 180°C., 350°F., Gas Mark 4.

94 MILLIONAIRE'S TART

8 ozs. flour.
Cayenne pepper.
Salt.
4 ozs. butter or margarine.
6 ozs. smoked salmon trimmings.
1 oz. butter.
1 small onion, finely chopped.
8 ozs. cream cheese.
3 eggs, size 3.
Nutmeg, salt and pepper.
8 oz. packet frozen spinach.

Make up shortcrust pastry, line 9 inch flan tin and bake blind.
Melt butter, cook onion slowly till very soft.
Tip into sieve, leave to drain and cool.
Beat onion into cream cheese with eggs and plenty of seasoning.
Cook spinach till thawed in very little water.
Drain thoroughly, squeeze out excess liquid.
Add to cheese mixture with chopped smoked salmon trimmings.
Spoon into flan case. Bake 30 – 35 minutes, moderate oven, till golden and puffed.
Cool then remove from tin.
Store overnight in fridge or freeze up to a month.
Reheat gently before serving.
One 9 inch tart makes 16 fingers.

95 MRS PROCKTER'S BREAKFAST PANCAKES

1 milk loaf.
2 eggs.
½ pint milk.
Maple or golden syrup.
Fat for frying.
Grilled bacon, sausages and tomatoes.

Beat the eggs and milk well together.
Slice the milk loaf into ½ inch thick rounds, soak these in the milk mixture, then fry until a golden brown on both sides.
Pile the slices on to a very hot dish and serve with maple syrup or golden syrup and grilled bacon and sausages and tomatoes.

96 SCALLOPED POTATOES

5 large potatoes.
1 onion.
1 pint milk.
Salt and pepper.
Flour.
Butter.

Grease a 3-pint casserole.
Slice potatoes thinly.
Grate onion.
Place potatoes in layers in casserole.
Sprinkle each layer with salt, pepper, flour and onion, dot with butter.
Heat the milk and pour over potatoes, dot with butter.
Cook in hot oven 200°C., 400°F., Gas Mark 6 for 1½ hours.

97 SMOKED HADDOCK SAVOURIES

4 ozs. cheese pastry:

4 ozs. flour.
2 ozs. grated cheese.
1¼ ozs. margarine.
1 egg yolk to bind.

Filling:

1 fillet cooked, flaked, smoked haddock.
1 yolk or beaten egg.
1 oz. butter.
Salt and pepper.
1 oz. grated cheese.

For the filling, melt butter, stir in fish, egg, cheese and seasoning. Cool.

Roll out the pastry thinly and cut into 2-inch rounds. Place small ball of filling in each circle. Dampen edges and fold into rectangular shapes. Pinch edges and brush with beaten egg. Bake at 180°C., 350°F., Gas Mark 4, for 10–15 minutes, until golden. Serve hot.

98 TASTY SUPPER DISH

2 sheep's kidneys.
2 round dinner rolls.
Butter or margarine.
Seasoning.

Cut the tops off the top of the rolls to form lids, butter them inside completely.

Skin and core the kidneys and pop inside the rolls with seasoning.

Place lids on top, bake in medium oven for 20 minutes.

Serves 2 people.

99 TOMATO WIGGLE

2 eggs.
2 tomatoes dropped in boiling water and skinned.
¼ teacup of bread-crumbs.
¼ lb. grated cheese.
2 ozs. margarine.
Season with salt and pepper.

Whisk eggs, chop tomatoes and mix with bread-crumbs and cheese, season rather lightly.

Leave in basin until wanted.

Melt a knob of margarine in saucepan and stir "wiggle" over the cooker until it is almost set.

Serve on toast.

The quantity makes two good portions.

100 TUNA AND SMOKED CHEESE FLAN

1 7 oz. tin tuna fish.
2 eggs.
7-inch flan ring lined with wholemeal pastry.
4 ozs. smoked cheese.
½ pint white sauce.

Bake lined flan blind till just set.
Flake tuna fish; add with ¾ grated cheese to white sauce. Beat in two egg yolks.
Whip egg whites till stiff, fold into fish mixture. Season.
Pour mixture into cooked flan, sprinkle rest of cheese over.
Bake in medium oven till well risen and golden. Serve immediately.

PUDDINGS AND SWEETS

101 ANGEL FOOD

(No cooking)

3 eggs.
4 ozs. caster sugar.
1 lemon or orange.
½ oz. gelatine.

Beat yolks of eggs and sugar to a thick light cream.
Add juice and finely grated rind of fruit.
Melt gelatine in ½ tumblerful hot water.
Whisk egg whites to a stiff froth.
Add gelatine to sugar and eggs, beat lightly till it becomes thick.
Quickly fold in whites and pour into a glass dish.

102 APPLE CRISP

1 oz. ground rice.
2 ozs. desiccated coconut.
1 level teaspoon baking powder.
2 ozs. margarine
2 ozs. caster sugar.
½ teaspoon almond essence.
1 lb. Bramley or other cooking apples.
2 tablespoons jam.
2 tablespoons sugar (for apples).

Peel, core and slice apples and stew with 2 tablespoons sugar until soft.
Sieve baking powder and ground rice together, add coconut.
Cream margarine and caster sugar until light, adding almond essence slowly.
Beat egg and add alternately with dry ingredients to the creamed mixture.
Grease a shallow fireproof dish and spread the jam over the bottom.
Place stewed apples over the jam then cover the apples with the creamed mixture.
Bake in a fairly hot oven 200°C., 400°F., Gas Mark 6 for 15–20 minutes or until top is crisp.

103 APPLE FLAN

Line a greased flan tin with short pastry.
Into this put grated apple, raisins, sprinkled sugar and a little powdered cinnamon in layers, finishing with apple.
Pour over this a few tablespoons of (melted) golden syrup.
Put a few knobs of butter on top, and bake for about 20 minutes.

104 APPLE SOUFFLÉ

2 ozs. sugar.
2 eggs.
4 tablespoons apple purée.
¾ pint milk.
1 dessertspoon gelatine.
2 to 3 tablespoons whipped cream.
The rind of 1 lemon.

Boil the milk with the lemon rind and strain on the egg yolks which have been worked with the sugar.
Add the gelatine and thicken over the fire without boiling.
Strain, and when cool fold in lightly the stiffly whipped egg whites, apple purée and two-thirds of the cream.
Put into small dishes and decorate with the rest of the cream when quite cold.

105 BANANA SURPRISE

A little jam.
1 pint milk.
2 heaped tablespoons semolina.
2 ozs. caster sugar.
Lemon essence.
2 large or 3 small bananas.
Lemon.
Desiccated coconut.

Make semolina mixture by taking a little of the milk and mixing cold with the semolina and the sugar.
Bring the remainder of the milk to the boil, pour on to the semolina mixture and add a few drops of lemon essence.
Return to the saucepan and cook slowly until whole thickens.
Stir well to avoid lumps.
Line the bottom of a pyrex dish with jam, preferably apricot.
Over this spread a layer of prepared semolina.

Slice bananas and thinly sprinkle with lemon juice, place these on semolina.
Cover with another layer of semolina mixture.
Sprinkle lightly with desiccated coconut and bake in a slow oven for 15 minutes or until pale brown.

106 BLACKBERRY CHARLOTTE

1 quart blackberries.
Stale bread.
1 pint custard.
½ oz. gelatine.
Butter and sugar.

Coat a mould with butter, line the sides with strips of bread (previously soaked in sweetened milk) and shape a piece to fit the bottom of the mould.
Place blackberries in stewpan, add sugar and gelatine (previously soaked in water), stir until dissolved.
Stew till tender, pour into mould, cover with pieces of bread, and put small plate on top.
Serve when cold and set, with custard poured round.

107 CHOCOLATE PUDDING

3½ ozs. plain chocolate.
1 pint milk.
1 oz. caster sugar.
Vanilla essence.
2 ozs. cornflour.
The juice of 2 lemons.
2 eggs.
A few almonds.

Mix cornflour to a smooth paste with a little milk, and add the melted chocolate.
Boil the milk and stir into the paste; stir over the heat till it thickens, boil gently for about 5 minutes.
Add the juice of lemon and the sugar, and let it cool.
Beat the yolks of eggs and add to the mixture.
Pour into a well buttered mould and cover with a buttered paper, and steam for ¾ hour.
Beat the whites of eggs to a stiff froth, add a few drops of vanilla essence and a dessertspoon caster sugar.
Turn the pudding out carefully and cover roughly with the whites, sprinkle with chopped almonds.
Put into the oven and brown slightly.

108 COFFEE FRIDGE CAKE

4 ozs. soft butter or margarine.
6 ozs. caster sugar.
4 eggs.
4 ozs. walnuts.
1 tablespoon coffee powder.
1 tablespoon milk.
1½ packets sponge cakes.
1 oz. whipping or double cream.

Cream butter, sugar and egg yolks.
Chop walnuts.
Dissolve coffee in milk, add to creamed mixture with two-thirds walnuts.
Whip egg-whites till stiff and add to creamed mixture.
Cut sponge cakes into thin slices and line a glass dish. Add a layer of mixture.
Do this till all mixture is used up, ending with a layer of sponge.
Cover and leave in fridge overnight or freeze overnight until needed.
Finish off with whipped cream and remaining nuts.

Juice and rind of a large lemon may be used instead of coffee.

109 CHEESECAKE

(Baked)

Filling:
8 ozs. cottage cheese.
3 ozs. sour cream.
1 oz. caster sugar.
1 beaten egg.
½ teaspoon vanilla essence.
1 tablespoon flour.

Base:
6 ozs. crushed digestive biscuits.
2 ozs. melted butter.

Top:
3 ozs. sour cream or yoghurt.
1 tablespoon sugar.
½ teaspoon vanilla essence.

Mix together biscuits and butter and press into bottom of 7-inch flan ring or tin with removeable bottom. Chill.
Mix filling ingredients together, stirring well, pour over biscuit base.
Bake for 25 minutes at 160°C., 320°F., Gas Mark 5, till set.
Remove from oven, turn oven up to max.
Mix ingredients for topping, spoon over cheesecake, return to oven for 5 minutes.
Topping sets as it cools. Decorate and serve.

110 CLEOPATRA PUDDINGS

For base:

2 ozs. caster sugar.
2 size 3 eggs and 2 yolks.
1 teaspoon lemon zest.
1 pint milk.

For topping:

Sponge cakes cut into rounds.
Sherry.
Raspberries.
Whipped cream.
5 ozs. caster sugar.
3 size 3 egg whites

Beat sugar, whole eggs, yolks and lemon zest together with fork in a bowl.

Scald milk and pour gently onto eggs and sugar mixture mixing all together gently.

Butter individual fireproof dishes and three-quarter fill these with custard mixture. Stand these in a roasting tin of water, cover with buttered greaseproof paper and cook in a moderate oven until set.

Remove from oven, cool a little, then place round of sponge cake on each custard. Pour over a little sherry sufficient to moisten cake.

Cover with raspberries mixed with whipped cream.

Whisk egg whites until stiff and then beat in caster sugar. Pipe or spoon meringue over raspberries and put in a slow oven until crisp.

111 DATE, APPLE AND CORNFLAKE PUDDING

Sliced apple.
Dates.
Brown sugar.
Lemon rind and juice.
Cornflakes.

Well grease a pie-dish and put layers of sliced apple on bottom.

Follow with chopped dates, brown sugar, lemon rind and juice and cornflakes.

Repeat layers until dish is full, finishing with a very thick covering of cornflakes.

Bake in a moderate oven for about ¾ hour.

112 DUTCH APPLE CAKE PUDDING

8 ozs. self-raising flour.
6 ozs. margarine.
4 ozs. sugar.
A pinch of salt.
2 large apples.
Swiss roll tin, well greased.
Sugar for sprinkling.
1 egg.

Rub in fat to flour, add sugar and salt.
Then mix to a stiff mixture with beaten egg.
Spread mixture on tin.
Arrange sliced apples in rows over pudding and lastly sprinkle with sugar.
Cook in moderate oven.
Delicious short appley pudding served with custard.

113 GERMAN APPLE TART

1½ lbs. apples, peeled and cored.
¼ lb. dates, washed, chopped and stoned.
½ teaspoon mixed spice, or cinnamon if preferred.
2 cups water.
¼ lb. brown sugar.

Stew all gently and strain off juice.
Line a cake tin with short pastry which has 2 ozs. brown sugar and a little spice in it.
Fill case with fruit when cold, cover with top well sealed, and cook.
Turn out upside down, pepper with icing sugar and a pinch of brown sugar in the middle before serving.
It is nicer eaten cold for teas, supper or parties.

114 GLAMOUR SWEET DISH

3 ozs. rice.
1 pint milk.
1 rounded teaspoon cornflour.
2 eggs.
2½ ozs. sugar.
½ teaspoon vanilla essence.
2 tablespoons jam.
A pinch of salt.

Wash rice and cook in the milk and salt until tender.
Blend cornflour with cold water, stir into rice and cook for 2 or 3 minutes.
Remove from heat, stir beaten egg yolks into mixture and add vanilla essence and 1 oz. sugar.
Pour into casserole and spread with jam.
Beat egg whites to a stiff froth, fold in most of the remaining sugar and pile on top of jam.
Decorate with cherries and angelica and dust with the rest of the sugar.
Bake in a slow oven for about ½ hour, or until set and slightly brown.

115 GINGER MERINGUE

1 round of Victoria Sandwich.
2–3 pieces of preserved stem ginger.
3½ ozs. caster sugar.
2–3 tablespoons of ginger syrup.
2 teaspoons lemon juice.
2 small egg whites.

Place cake in a round ovenproof dish to fit.
Prick cake all over with a fork.
Mix ginger syrup and lemon juice and pour over cake slowly so that it sinks in.
Chop ginger finely and strew over cake.
Whisk egg whites until stiff, whisk in half of the sugar, then fold in remainder.
Spread meringue over cake and ginger, and rough up surface.
Bake in a hot oven 190°C., (375°C., Gas Mark 5) for about 10 minutes.
It should brown, but not burn.

116 ONE OF GRANDMA'S SWEETS

3 or 4 oranges, peel and cut thinly.

Place a layer of orange in a glass dish and sprinkle with caster sugar and desiccated coconut.
Then another layer of orange, sugar and coconut.
Leave for 3 to 4 hours.
Can be served with cornflour sauce.
Serve when cold.

117 HAZELNUT MERINGUE GATEAU

4 ozs. hazelnuts.
4 egg whites.
¼ pint double cream.
3 tablespoons milk.
8 ozs. caster sugar.
1 teaspoon white vinegar.
1½ ozs. butter.
1 oz. cocoa.
4 ozs. icing sugar.

Place nuts on tray, put in moderately hot oven for a few minutes. Tip on to a clean teatowel, rub off skins. Place in blender and grind.
Lightly brush the sides of two 8 inch-sandwich tins with oil and line the base with non stick parchment.
Whisk the egg whites till stiff. Whisk in ½ sugar, a spoonful at a time, until meringue is glossy. Mix the ground hazelnuts with the remaining sugar and fold into the meringue with the vinegar. Divide the mixture between the tins.
Spread flat and bake in a moderate oven for 45 minutes. Then turn off the heat and leave to cool in the oven. Remove, turn out and peel off parchment.
Whisk cream till thick. Melt butter in small saucepan, stir in cocoa and cook gently for 1 minute. Stir in milk and icing sugar. Mix well to a thick spreading consistency and spread over 1 half of the meringue. Spread the cream on the other half, sandwich together.

To freeze. Open freeze, then pack in large rigid polythene container.
To serve. Place on a serving dish and thaw for at least 12 hours in the refrigerator. Dust with a little icing sugar and decorate with chocolate flake before serving.
Cooking time 45 minutes. Oven setting 180°C., 350°F., Gas Mark 4.

118 HAZELNUT FLAN

5 tablespoons sugar.
½ teacup milk.
¼ lb. ground hazelnuts.
8 ozs. flour.
2½ ozs. sugar.
5 ozs. margarine.

Put sugar in a saucepan and brown over heat.
Add about ½ teacup milk, stirring all the time, and let the mixture come to the boil.
Stir in the ground hazelnuts.

Leave to cool.
Sieve together the flour and sugar and rub in the margarine.
Then knead to make pastry and roll out to line and cover a flan tin.
Put in the mixture and bake till golden brown in a moderate oven for about 20 minutes.

119 ICED CURRANTS

¼ pint water.
Currants.
2 egg whites.
Caster sugar.

Select fine clusters of red, white or black currants.
Well beat the egg whites and mix with the water.
Take the currants, a cluster at a time, and dip them in.
Drain for a moment, then roll or shake them in the caster sugar.
Lay them to dry on clean kitchen paper, when the sugar will crystalise round each currant, giving a very pretty effect.
All fresh fruit may be prepared in this way and attractively arranged on one dish makes an excellent summer dessert.

120 KONFIT SHORTBREAD

Mix together a saltspoon of salt, ½ teaspoon of bicarbonate of soda, a teaspoonful of cream of tartar.
Stir these into 1 lb. of flour, add 2 ozs. rice flour.
Now rub ½ lb. butter into the flour to make a paste.
Divide into two portions, roll out and bake.
Put a thick layer of jam or marmalade between, and replace the other on top.
Serve hot with cream on top.

121 LEMON FLUFF

3 eggs.
2 lemons.
2 dessertspoons cornflour.
2 cupfuls water.
1 cupful sugar.

Mix cornflour with water and sugar, add beaten yolks of eggs, juice of lemons and rind of 1 lemon.
Boil till it thickens, and mix with stiffly-beaten whites of eggs.
Serve cold.

122 LEMON MERINGUES

1 lemon.
Water.
2 dessertspoons sugar.
1 egg.
2 dessertspoons cornflour.

Put the grated rind of lemon and juice into a saucepan, making juice up to a good ½ pint with water.
Mix the cornflour with a little of the liquid and add to saucepan.
Stir over fire until mixture thickens and is cooked.
Separate white of egg from yolk.
When the contents of pan have cooled add yolk and cook for 1 minute.
Place in small glasses.
Beat up white of egg with 2 ozs. caster sugar until very stiff.
Place on top of lemon mixture and put back in a slow oven lightly to colour and set meringue.

Red currant juice or loganberry juice instead of lemon makes a delicious sweet made like the above.

123 LEMON PUDDING

1 tablespoon butter (2 ozs.)
½ cup sugar.
1 cup milk.
2 eggs.
2 large tablespoons self-raising flour.
1 lemon.

Carry out *in this order:*
Cream butter and sugar.
Sift in flour, then the juice and grated rind of lemon, then yolks of eggs and the milk, beating between each addition.
Lastly fold in stiffly beaten whites of eggs.
Pour into a greased pie-dish and set dish in a tin of water in a moderate oven.
Bake for about 30 minutes when pudding should consist of a light sponge top with lemon cream at the bottom.

124 LEMON CRUNCH

Filling:
Finely grated rind of 2 lemons (plus juice made up with pint of water).
1 oz. cornflour.
1 whole egg and 1 yolk.
2 ozs. sugar.

Base:
2 ozs. butter.
2 ozs. plain chocolate.
6 ozs. crushed digestive biscuits.

Topping:
¼ pint double cream.
1 egg white.

Well oil inside a 7-inch flan ring. Put it on a flat serving dish.
Melt butter and chocolate together, stir in biscuits and mix well.
Press crumbs into oiled ring and flatten for base.
Blend cornflour and some of the liquid. Boil remainder of liquid and stir into the cornflour.
Stir mixture over heat till thickened. Mix in sugar, beat in the eggs and extra yolk. Leave to cool.
Pour on to biscuit base, place in fridge till set. Lift off flan ring.
Whip cream till just thick, whisk egg white to firm hold, fold into cream. Pipe over filling and decorate.

125 LEMON TART

1 large cooking apple.
1 lemon
1 egg.
¾ cup sugar.
4 ozs. short crust pastry.

Peel and grate apple.
Add sugar and grated rind and juice of lemon.
Beat egg, add to apple mixture; mix well.
Line a 7-inch tart plate with pastry.
Add the filling and bake in a moderate oven for 25 – 30 minutes.
Serve cold with cream or custard.

126 MARZIPAN MIXTURE

(For Maids of Honour Tartlets)

Mix together:
2 tablespoons caster sugar.
2 tablespoons ground almonds.
1 tablespoon cornflour.
1 egg, unbeaten.
A few drops of essence of almonds.

127 *MINIATURE RICE PUDDINGS*

¼ lb. rice.
1½ pints milk.
2 ozs. butter.
4 eggs.
Sugar to taste.
1 lemon.
Almond or vanilla flavouring.
A few strips of candied peel.

Allow rice to simmer with a strip of lemon in 1 pint of milk until tender.
Then stir in the butter and other ½ pint of milk and let the mixture cool.
Then add the well beaten eggs and a few drops of essence (whichever is preferred).
Grease some small cups or moulds and line with a few thin slices of candied peel, then fill three parts full with the mixture.
Bake for 40 minutes in moderate oven.
Turn out and serve with custard or sweet sauce.

The flavouring and candied peel might be omitted, and stewed fruit or preserve served instead with these puddings.

128 *TRADITIONAL RICE PUDDING*

2 ozs. short grain rice.
1 pint milk.
2 level tablespoons sugar.

Either put all the ingredients in a pyrex dish and bake for one hour in a moderate oven, stirring mixture once through during cooking.
Or put all the ingredients in top of double boiler and cook very gently until creamy, for two hours.
If done in a single thick based pan, allow 30 minutes.

129 *MOCK MOUSSE*

½ pint undiluted orange squash or fruit purée.
½ pint water.
1 tablespoon semolina.
1 tablespoon sugar.
½ oz. gelatine.
Cream for garnishing.

Mix all the ingredients together.
Put into a pan and bring to the boil, stirring all the time.
Boil for 1 minute, and then pour into a bowl.
Allow to semi-set.
Whip for ¼ hour.
Allow to set in the container or bowl in which it is to be served.
Garnish with cream.

130 NEW PLUM TART

Stew ½ lb. plums and rub through a sieve.
Line a cake tin with short crust pastry and put in the plum purée.
Whip the white of an egg with ½ cup of caster sugar.
Beat in 1 tablespoon of ground rice and 2 ozs. ground almonds.
Place on top of plum purée.
Bake in a moderate oven.

131 PINEAPPLE WHIP

2 eggs.
½ oz. gelatine.
2 ozs. caster sugar.
1 small tin pineapple and the juice.
½ pint cream.

Mix sugar with egg yolks.
Melt gelatine in pineapple juice over gentle heat and add to egg and sugar mixture and let it cool.
When cool, whisk until it starts to thicken, and add cream, whipped.
Finally, add whisked whites of egg and lastly the pineapple, keeping a few pieces out for decoration.

132 PAVLOVA

3 large egg whites.
6 ozs. caster sugar.
1 level teaspoon vinegar.
1 level teaspoon cornflour.

Whip egg whites till stiff.
Fold in caster sugar with metal spoon.
Add cornflour and vinegar.
Whip further minute to blend.
Pipe out around onto parchment paper or non stick paper on baking tray.
Pipe remainder into small rounds in similar way and cook till dry in very low oven.
Place small rounds on edge of circle. Decorate and fill with whipped cream and fresh fruit.

133 PRINCESS PUDDING

- 6 ozs. stoned dates.
- 3 ozs. dried apricots (not soaked)
- 2 fresh moderate-sized bananas.
- Grated rind of 2 lemons.
- 2 eggs.

Put dates, apricots and bananas through a mincer alternately.
Place in a basin, add the lemon rind and mix in well.
Whisk egg yolks and whites separately then add to fruit and beat for a few minutes.
Grease a basin, put in the mixture, and steam gently for 1 hour.

134 SAGO PLUM PUDDING

- 1 breakfastcup of chopped raisins.
- 1 breakfastcup of bread-crumbs.
- 1 breakfastcup of moist sugar.
- 4 heaped tablespoons small sago.
- ½ pint milk.
- 1 oz. butter.
- ½ teaspoon bicarbonate of soda.
- Grated rind of 1 lemon.

Soak sago in milk overnight.
Then mix well with other ingredients.
Put into basin and boil for 3 hours.

135 TO COOK RHUBARB

Cut up in 1 inch pieces.
Place in a fireproof dish (that has a cover).
Add a cup of sugar to the pound of rhubarb (approximately).
Leave overnight.
Then carefully cook in own juice, in a slow oven.

136 SWISS CREAM

1 pint milk or cream.
1 teaspoon cornflour.
6 ozs. sugar.
The juice of 2 lemons.
Some macaroons.

Boil milk or cream with the cornflour and sugar.
When cold add the lemon juice and pour over macaroons.

137 STRAWBERRY LAYER GATEAU

6 ozs. butter or margarine.
3 eggs.
5½–6 ozs. SR flour.
6 ozs. caster sugar.
1½ ozs. ground almonds.
Pinch of salt.

Filling and decoration:
1 lb. strawberries.
½ pint of double cream, lightly whipped.

Grease 2, 8-inch sandwich tins, line the base with greaseproof. Cream butter and sugar till light and fluffy, gradually beat in eggs with almonds. Sieve in flour. Turn into tins and bake in moderate oven 20–25 minutes, 180°C., 350°F., Gas Mark 4.

Leave in tins for few minutes, turn out and cool. Halve or quarter strawberries. Spread one third of cream on top of one cake and half of strawberries. Sandwich cakes together, spread half remaining cream on top. Pipe remainder and decorate with strawberries.

138 TEACUP PUDDING

A the bottom of a buttered dish put in layers:

A teacupful each of bread-crumbs, currants, suet, and sugar.

Beat the yolks of 2 eggs and the white of 1, and pour roughly over.
Bake for ½ hour in moderate oven.

139 TREACLE GEORGE

Butter a pie-dish and line the bottom with thin short pastry.
Spread with a good layer of golden syrup and fine white bread-crumbs.
Add a sprinkle of lemon juice.
Fill up the dish with layers of pastry, syrup and crumbs, sprinkling each layer with a few drops of lemon juice.
Bake in a fairly quick oven for ¾ hour.
Serve hot or cold with clotted cream.

140 PINEAPPLE UPSIDE-DOWN PUDDING

3 ozs. flour.
4 ozs. butter.
4 ozs sugar.
1 egg.
1 small tin pineapple.

Mix sugar and butter to cream.
Use rather less than half to line bottom and sides of dish.
Into remainder of butter add flour and beaten egg.
Lay pineapple in bottom of dish, then pour batter on top.
Bake for about ½ hour in moderate oven.

If egg is not sufficient for making batter, use a little pineapple juice.
Make sauce with juice and custard powder, same method as for custard.
Turn pudding out on to dish before serving, pineapple thus coming upwards.

141 TOBY'S CHOCOLATE PUDDING

3 ozs. self-raising flour.
2 level tablespoons cocoa powder (or Cadbury's Drinking Chocolate).
Pinch salt.
4 ozs. butter or margarine.
4 ozs. caster sugar.
2 eggs.
½ teaspoon vanilla essence.
1 tablespoon chopped walnuts.
1–2 tablespoons milk.

For the Sauce

4 ozs. soft brown sugar.
2 level tablespoons cocoa or chocolate powder.
½ pint hot water.

Sift together the flour, cocoa powder and salt. Cream the butter or margarine and sugar until light. Lightly mix the eggs and vanilla essence and gradually beat into the creamed mixture. Add a little of the sifted flour with the last few additions of egg and then fold in the remaining flour, walnuts and enough milk to mix to a medium soft consistency. Spoon the mixture into a well buttered 2 or 2½ pint dish and spread evenly. Set aside while preparing the sauce.

In a mixing basin, combine together the soft brown sugar and cocoa or chocolate powder. Stir in the hot water and mix well. Pour over the top of the cake mixture. Place the pudding at once just above centre in a moderately hot oven 190°C., (375°F., or Gas Mark 5) and bake for 40 minutes. During baking, the cake will rise to the top and the baked pudding will have a delicious chocolate sauce underneath.

Serve hot with cream or ice cream. Serves 4.

142 VELVET CREAM

1 jelly.
½ gill water.
1 small tin evaporated milk.

Dissolve the jelly in the hot water and leave to cool.
Beat the milk to a stiff cream.
Add the cool jelly and beat well together.
Put aside to set in individual dishes, cap with real cream and cherry.

143 WALNUT CREAM FLAN

Make a Sponge Flan as follows:

(1) Whisk together—
    3 small or 2 large eggs, with
    3 ozs. caster sugar, and
    Finely grated rind of ½ a lemon.
  Until thick and creamy.

(2) To this fold in with metal spoon—
    1½ ozs. melted butter.
    3 ozs. self-raising flour.
  These should be folded in alternately, half at a time.
  Pour into well greased flan tin and bake for 20 – 25 minutes.

When cold, fill with following filling:

(1) Cream together—
    4 ozs. butter.
    6 ozs. caster sugar.

(2) Beat in 2 eggs.

(3) Add 2 ozs. finely chopped walnuts and a few drops vanilla.
Leave for 24 hours, and decorate with angelica and crystallised violets.

Serve with HOT chocolate sauce.

144 STEAMED SYRUP SPONGE

4 tablespoons golden syrup.
6 ozs. margarine.
6 ozs. caster sugar.
6 ozs. self-raising flour.
3 large eggs.

Grease pudding basin and put warmed syrup in the bottom.
Cream margarine and sugar together.
Blend in beaten eggs and sifted flour.
Pour mixture over syrup in the bowl.
Cover top with greased greaseproof paper with pleat in it. Fold down edges.
Steam in a double steamer on medium speed for 1½ hours.
Serve with either custard or cream and extra golden syrup.

145 CHOCOLATE MOCHA SAUCE

2 rounded tablespoons drinking chocolate.
1 heaped teaspoon instant coffee.
1 rounded tablespoon cornflour.
2 ozs. golden syrup.

Mix chocolate, coffee and cornflour with a little cold water, to a cream.
Add hot water to make 11 ozs. Add syrup and cook gently until thickened.

146 CHOCOLATE GINGER SAUCE

2 rounded tablespoons drinking chocolate (fat-reduced if available).
2 tablespoons ginger syrup.
5 pieces stem ginger, chopped.
1 rounded tablespoon cornflour.

Blend these together and make up to 12 fluid ounces with water or milk.
Heat gently, stirring until sauce is thickened.
If wanted to use cold, add 1 oz. more liquid.

147 WITCHES' CREAM

(It's Wizard!)

Soften 1 heaped teaspoon gelatine in about ½ cup of water.
Into a bowl put the juice of 2 lemons, grated rind of 1 lemon, 3 ozs. sugar and 3 egg yolks.
Whisk over steam until thick, then add gelatine and whisk (with bowl standing in cold water) until cool.
Fold in the 3 egg whites beaten stiff with 1 tablespoon icing sugar added *or* 2 egg whites and ¼ pint whipped cream.
Pile into sundae glasses and sprinkle with a few chopped toasted almonds.
Serve with sponge fingers or thin biscuits.

CAKES AND BISCUITS

148 ALMOND CAKE

4 eggs.
¼ lb. caster sugar.
½ lb. ground almonds.

Stir the yolks of eggs and sugar together with the almonds.
Add the stiffly whipped whites of eggs.
Stir all together and bake in a moderate oven.

149 APPLE CAKE

12 ozs. peeled apple, diced.
5 ozs. soft margarine.
8 ozs. self-raising flour.
1½ teaspoons baking powder.
8 ozs. sugar.
2 eggs.
½ teaspoon lemon juice.

Put all ingredients in basin, except apple, and beat together.
Grease an 8-inch tin, put half mixture in tin, put apple on top, then rest of the mixture.
Smooth over the top. Sprinkle with flaked almonds.
Bake 1½ hours at 160°C., 325°F., Gas Mark 3.

150 BROWN COOKIES

1 breakfastcup Quaker Oats.
1 breakfastcup flour.
1 breakfastcup coconut.
¼ lb. butter.
1 egg.
1 small cup sugar.
1 tablespoon golden syrup.
1 teaspoon bicarbonate of soda.

Rub butter into dry ingredients, then add golden syrup, add egg.
If mixed with hand no milk is needed.
Place in small heaps on a greased tin and bake in a slow oven.

151 A USEFUL CAKE FILLING

If you have any left over cold custard, mix with icing sugar, and it makes a very nice filling for sponges.

152 CARROT AND ALMOND CAKE

- 8 ozs. margarine.
- 8 ozs. sugar (half caster half soft brown).
- 4 eggs, beaten with one teaspoon orange-flower water.
- 8 ozs. freshly grated carrot.
- 2 ozs. ground almonds
- 8 ozs. self-raising flour (white, mixed with up to 50% wholemeal).
- 1–2 ozs. flaked or chopped almonds.
- 3 teaspoons demerara sugar.

Cream margarine and sugar well until very light. Mix together egg mixture, carrot and ground almonds and blend into creamed mixture. Fold in flour mixture. Mix in some top of milk if the wholemeal flour makes cake batter too dry, or just use larger eggs.
Grease and line a roasting tin or large cake tin and spread cake batter in this, levelling the top lightly. Sprinkle over with the flaked/chopped almonds and demerara sugar.
Bake in a moderate oven, 350°F., 180°C., Gas Mark 4, for about 45 minutes, till cake springs back when pressed with the fingertips.
Cool and cut into 24 or 32 pieces. The cake can also keep well in the freezer as a large slab. (A delicious cake, which sold well at fairs or fetes at 10p per piece when cut into 24 pieces).

153 CARROT AND CIDER CAKE

- 8 ozs. S.R. flour (or 6 ozs. white and 2 ozs. wholemeal).
- 4 ozs. butter or margarine.
- 4 ozs. moist brown sugar.
- 1 tablespoon golden syrup.
- 4 ozs. mixed fruit.
- 2 medium carrots.
- ½ teaspoon mixed spice.
- ¼ pint medium dry cider.
- 1 egg.
- A little milk if needed.

Sieve flour, add pinch salt, rub fat into flour until like breadcrumbs.
Stir in sugar and spice.
Mince or process carrots finely, add with fruit to flour.
Whisk egg, stir in and add cider and syrup.
Add a little milk and mix to a dropping consistency.
Place in a well greased 7½ by 4½ loaf tin.
Place greased paper or foil in bottom.
Cook in middle of oven 1½ hours Gas Mark 3, 175°C., 325°F.

154 CHINESE CHEWS

2 eggs.
1 cup sugar.
¾ cup self-raising flour.
1 cup walnuts.
1 cup dates.

Mix all together and spread thin on a well-buttered tin.
When done, cut in squares and roll in powdered sugar.

155 STEAMED CHOCOLATE CAKE OR PUDDING

(No egg—no oven)

Sieve together:
- 5 ozs. self-raising flour.
- 1 oz. caster sugar.
- 1 oz. cocoa powder.
- ½ teaspoon bicarbonate of soda.

and warm over a low heat:
- 2 ozs. margarine.
- Good tablespoon treacle.
- 3 tablespoons milk.
- 3 tablespoons water.

Pour this tepid mixture over the flour mixture and mix gradually to a smooth batter.
Turn into a greased 5 inch cake tin, cover with grease paper, and steam covered closely for 1 hour.
Leave cake in tin to dry off for a few minutes, then cool on a wire tray.
Do not cut for at least 24 hours.

Note: This will cook just as well in a basin and is delicious with icing set on top and running over. Children love this.

156 CHOCOLATE CRISPS

5 ozs. granulated sugar.
3 ozs. margarine.
2 ozs. lard.
2 ozs. cocoa.
8 ozs. self-raising flour.

Rub well together, knead and work in the palms of your hands, 1 dessertspoonful at a time till a round flat cake is formed.
Place well apart on a greased tin and bake slowly till crisp and *hard in centre.* This last is important.

157 CHOCOLATE DATE CAKE

1 packet cooking dates and hot water.
½ cup top of 1 pint milk.
1 tablespoon cocoa powder, *or* 2 of cooking chocolate.
2 cups demerara sugar.
½ cup butter *or* margarine.
2 cups of flour.
1½ teaspoons baking powder, if plain flour used.
½ teaspoon cinnamon..
2 egg yolks.

Cover dates with boiling water.
Melt cocoa, cream and 1 cup sugar in a saucepan.
Cream together 1 cup sugar and fat.
Sift flour and baking powder and add to creamed mixture.
Beat in egg yolks, 1 at a time.
Mix date and chocolate mixtures and add.
Bake in a tin 7 inches in diameter in a moderate oven, 325 degrees F. for ½ hour, and lower to 225 degrees F. for ½ hour more or till cooked.

158 CHOCOLATE TRUFFLES

4½ ozs. powdered chocolate.
2 ozs. butter.
2 egg yolks (2 ozs. ground almonds may be added if wished).
2 ozs. sifted icing sugar.
¾ teaspoon vanilla essence.
A few drops of coffee essence.

Beat the egg yolks.
Cream butter and sugar.
Mix all ingredients together into a thick paste.
Shape into balls and roll each in chocolate.

159 OLD ENGLISH CIDER CAKE

8 ozs. plain flour.
½ teaspoon ginger.
½ teaspoon bicarbonate of soda.
Pinch of nutmeg.
4 ozs. butter.
4 ozs. caster sugar.
2 eggs.
¼ pint cider.

Sift dry ingredients, except sugar.
Cream butter and sugar until fluffy.
Beat in eggs, stir in half dry ingredients.
Add cider (previously whisked till frothy).
Add rest of dry ingredients; beat well.
Cook in a well greased shallow tin, 8 inches by 6 inches.
Bake in centre of oven at 325°F., 170°C., Gas Mark 3 for 45 minutes.
Leave at least 1 day before cutting.

160 CRUNCHY COOKIES

8 ozs. S.R. flour.
4 ozs. caster sugar.
4 ozs. soft margarine.
2 tablespoons coconut.
2 tablespoons grated chocolate.
2 tablespoons crushed walnuts.
1 egg.
½ level teaspoon bicarbonate of soda.

Mix to a soft dough, and with floured hands, take pieces the size of a walnut. Roll into a ball, flatten slightly and place on a baking sheet, leaving room for them to spread. Cook at 350°F., 180°C., Gas Mark 4 for 20 minutes.

161 COCONUT BUNS

1 lb. plain flour.
½ lb. desiccated coconut.
½ lb. margarine.
2 teaspoons baking powder.
10 ozs. caster sugar.
Pinch salt.
A little milk and egg.

Prepare by the rubbing in method.
Add beaten egg and enough milk to make a fairly stiff consistency.
Bake in a moderate oven.
This recipe can be halved.

162 COCONUT PYRAMIDS

1 teacup coconut.
½ cup sugar (caster).
1 egg.

Beat egg.
Add sugar and coconut and mix into a stiff paste.
Place on well buttered sheet into pyramid shape and bake in oven 375 degrees F. for about ½ hour.
This produces 1 dozen pyramids.

163 COCONUT WHISPERS

5 ozs. margarine and a good tablespoon of golden syrup melted gently together.
Beat well with 8 ozs. self-raising flour.
2 ozs. coconut.
5 ozs. granulated sugar.
1 well beaten egg in a little milk.

Makes 2 dozen small buns if baked in moderate oven.

164 CREAM SPONGE

2 large eggs.
4 ozs. self-raising flour.
4 ozs. sugar.
1 oz. butter.
1 dessertspoonful golden syrup.
2 tablespoons water.
A pinch of salt.

Beat eggs well, add sugar and beat until thick.
Stir in the flour, and add the melted butter, syrup and water.
Bake in sandwich tins, which have been well greased and the bottoms lined with greaseproof paper, in a moderate oven for 15–20 minutes.
When cold, sandwich together with whipped cream.

165 DATE AND WALNUT LOAF

8 ozs. wholemeal self-raising flour.
6 ozs. soft margarine.
8 ozs. light soft brown sugar.
8 ozs walnuts, chopped fine.
8 ozs. dates, chopped.
4 eggs, size 2.

Line 2 loaf tins (8½″ x 4¼″) with greaseproof paper.

Cream margarine and sugar together and beat in the eggs. Fold in the flour, then dates and nuts. Divide mixture between the 2 tins, smooth out with a slight hollow in the middle. Bake for about 45 minutes at 180°C., (350°F., Gas Mark 4).

166 FLAPJACKS

4 ozs. margarine.
6 ozs. rolled oats.
4 ozs sugar.
½ teaspoon almond essence.
A few almonds or any other nuts (optional).

Melt margarine in a saucepan.
Add (off the stove) sugar and oats, and almond essence.
Press lightly into greased sandwich tin, and sprinkle nuts on top.
Bake in a moderate oven for about 15 minutes.
Leave in tin till cold.
Cut into 8 triangular sections.

167 FARMHOUSE CAKE

½ lb. wholemeal flour.
½ lb. plain white flour.
½ teaspoon spice.
½ teaspoon bicarb.
6 ozs. butter or margarine.
½ lb. light brown sugar.
¼ lb. sultanas.
¼ lb. raisins.
1 oz. candied peel.
1 beaten egg.
Milk to mix.

Rubbing-in method. 8-inch tin. Moderate oven 1½ hours.

168 GINGERBREAD CAKE

(Keeps fresh for six months in a closed tin)

1 lb. plain flour (*not* self-raising).
½ lb. granulated sugar.
1 level teaspoon mixed spice.
1 teaspoon powdered ginger. } (use Apostle teaspoons)
Sieve all these and put into a big basin.

½ lb. golden syrup.
½ lb. margarine (Stork for preference).
Melt these in a small pan on the gas.

1 teacupful milk.
1 teaspoon bicarbonate of soda. } (mixed together).
2 ozs. crystal ginger.
2 ozs. mixed nuts.
2 ozs. dates, stoned and chopped.
1 egg.

Into the dry things pour the heated syrup and margarine and mix well.
Add fruit and nuts, and *one* beaten egg.
Lastly add milk and bicarbonate of soda, and mix well.
Pour into a buttered 3 lb. tin and put into slow oven for 1¾ or 2 hours.
Do not look at it for 1½ hours unless you smell it.

169 GINGERBREAD

½ lb. margarine.
1 lb. syrup.
6 ozs. demerara sugar.
3 eggs.
2 tablespoons milk (about).
1 lb. self-raising flour.
1 tablespoon marmalade.
2 tablespoons ginger.
2 teaspoons mixed spice.
½ teaspoon bicarbonate of soda.

Line tin with paper.
Melt margarine, syrup, sugar, marmalade and milk in a saucepan. *Do not boil.*
Put flour in large bowl with spice, ginger and bicarb.
Beat eggs and add, and then stir in contents of saucepan.
Bake in a moderate oven, 350°F., 180°C., Gas Mark 4, for ¾ to 1 hour.

170 MOIST GINGERBREAD

½ lb. flour.
3 ozs. sugar.
1 teaspoon ground ginger.
5 ozs. lard.
6 ozs. syrup (cup).
1 egg.

Melt sugar, lard and syrup.
Pour into flour and ginger.
Add egg.
Put quickly into greased baking tin about 6 inches by 9 inches.
Cook in *very* slow oven.
Cut in squares.

171 GLACÉ FRUIT CAKE

12 ozs. flour (half self-raising, half plain).
8 ozs. glacé cherries.
6 ozs. glacé pineapple.
2 ozs. crystallised ginger.
2 ozs. citron peel.
3 ozs. angelica.
8 ozs. butter.
8 ozs caster sugar.
1 lemon, juice and rind.
3 or 4 eggs.
8 ozs. sultanas.
2 ozs. chopped walnuts.
3 tablespoons sherry.
A little salt.

Cake tin 8 inches by 8½ inches.

Beat butter and sugar, cut all fruits not too small, and add other ingredients and bake 3 or 4 hours.
Oven 375°F., 190°C., Gas Mark 5 for 20 minutes, and reduce to 300°F., 150°C., Gas Mark 2.

172 GROUND RICE CAKE

4 ozs. butter.
1 breakfastcup sugar.
1 breakfastcup self-raising flour.
1 teacup ground rice.
2 eggs.
A pinch of baking powder.
A little milk if needed.

Beat the butter and sugar, add well beaten eggs, and gradually other ingredients, and beat well.
Prepare a tin 7 inches by 5 inches with greaseproof paper, and bake in oven for 1 hour.
Oven 375°F., 190°C., Gas Mark 5 for 20 minutes, and then turn oven to 300°F., 150°C., Gas Mark 2, and bake 1 hour in all.

173 ICEBOX COOKIES

1 cup margarine.
1½ cups brown sugar.
2 eggs.
½ cup chopped nuts *or* coconut (optional).
3 cups flour.
¼ teaspoon salt.
1 teaspoon baking powder.
1 teaspoon vanilla.

Cream fat and sugar, cream very light.
Add well beaten eggs, then sifted dry ingredients, lastly vanilla and nuts.
Form into rolls about 2 inches in diameter.
Wrap in greaseproof and chill in fridge or as cold a place as possible overnight.
Slice very thinly and bake in a moderate 350°F., 180°C., Gas Mark 4 for 10 minutes.

174 IRISH CAKE
(A very old recipe)

Short pastry.
Marmalade.
1 tablespoon margarine.
2 tablespoons caster sugar.
½ teaspoon almond essence.
1 or 2 eggs.
2 tablespoons coconut.

Line a sponge tin with pastry.
Place a layer of marmalade over pastry.
Beat sugar and margarine to a cream.
Add the egg or eggs and beat well.
Add almond essence and then coconut.
Spread mixture over marmalade.
Bake in a moderate oven.
Watch carefully whilst baking to prevent burning.
Serve cold.

175 LARD CAKE

Take a piece of proved dough and roll it flat into a square.
Dab pats of *lard* all over the dough.
Scatter over this some brown sugar, sultanas and currants.
You can also use grated nutmeg, spice, cinnamon, chopped peel—whatever the family likes and in any combination you like.
Then fold the corners into the centre like an envelope and then fold in half.
Roll flat again and repeat the whole process twice more.
Put into a greased tin and bake in a hot oven.
This mixture can also be cut into small squares or oblongs and baked on a baking sheet in a hot oven.

176 LEMON JUMBLES

¾ lb. self-raising flour.
4 ozs. caster sugar.
2 or 3 ozs. butter.
1 large lemon.
1 egg.
A little milk.

Cream the butter, add sugar and grated lemon rind.
Mix well and stir in the egg and strained lemon juice.
Sieve the flour and stir in lightly, using a little milk if necessary in order to make a rather stiff dough.
Turn on to a floured board and divide into small pieces, equal in size.
Roll each one out gently with the hands and twist into an S-shape.
Bake 15 to 20 minutes on a greased tin in a moderate oven.

177 LEMON OATIES

4 ozs. S.R. flour.
4 ozs. caster sugar.
4 ozs. porridge oats.
4 ozs. desiccated coconut.
4 ozs. margarine.
Grated rind of ½ lemon.
1 level tablespoon golden syrup.
2 level tablespoons water.
Juice of 1 lemon. } topping.
4 ozs. caster sugar. }

Swiss roll tin 8 inches by 12 inches approximately.

Place dry ingredients in bowl.
Cut fat into small pieces, rub in lightly.
Stir in golden syrup and water and press into a ball.
Turn mixture into greased tin and smooth out with hands.
Bake on centre shelf at 300°F., 150°C., Gas Mark 2, until golden brown.
Meanwhile mix topping to a thin paste.
When traybake is cooked, remove from oven and immediately spread the lemon and sugar mixture over the surface.
Cool before cutting into fingers.

178 MADEIRA CAKE

5 ozs. butter.
5 ozs. caster sugar.
1 teaspoon lemon rind, finely grated.
3 eggs.
6 ozs. self-raising flour.
1 tablespoon milk if needed.

Cream butter and sugar until light and fluffy. Add lemon rind.
Beat in the eggs a little at a time, fold in the flour then add enough milk (if needed) to give a soft dropping consistency.
Turn mixture into a greased and lined 6-inch cake tin.
Cook in a moderate oven 180°C. (350°F., Gas Mark 4) for 1 hour or

until golden brown, opening the oven door after 30 minutes to put a slice of citron peel gently on top.
Leave in the tin for 5 minutes, then turn out and cool on a wire rack.

Replace 1 oz. flour with 1 oz. cornflour or ground rice flour for a finer texture.

179 MARBLE CAKE

Cream together 6 ozs. margarine and 8 ozs. caster sugar.
Beat 4 or 5 eggs well, and add beaten eggs and 1 lb. flour alternately, until the flour is used up.
Divide the mixture into 3 separate basins, and add 1 teaspoonful baking powder to each (if plain flour is used).
Colour 1 section with cochineal, 1 with cocoa, and leave the third plain.
Grease a cake tin well and put in, first, a tablespoon of the plain, next 1 of the cocoa mixture, and then 1 of the pink mixture.
Continue in this way until all the mixture is used up.
Bake in a moderate oven for 1½ hours.
When cut, the cake has an attractive marbled appearance.

180 MELTING MOMENTS

2½ ozs. lard.
1½ ozs. margarine.
3 ozs. caster sugar.
½ egg.
4 ozs. self-raising flour.
½ teaspoon vanilla essence.

Make by creaming method, then roll mixture into balls about the size of a walnut.
Dampen slightly with water and roll in porridge oats.
Flatten and put a piece of glacé cherry in centre.
Bake in a moderate oven until nicely brown.

181 MELTING SNOWS

2 ozs. icing sugar.
2 ozs. custard powder.
6 ozs. margarine.
6 ozs. plain flour.

Cream margarine, add other ingredients.
Knead till pliable.
Roll into small balls.
Flatten with fork.
Bake in moderate oven, sandwich together with butter icing.

182 MRS MORGAN'S SPECIALS

2 tablespoons margarine.
1 cup sugar.
1 egg.
½ cup coconut.
1 cup mixed fruit.
1 cup self-raising flour.
Corn flakes.

Beat margarine and sugar to a cream.
Then add egg, coconut, mixed fruit and flour.
Mix well.
Take small quantities (about dessertspoonful) of mixture, roll in corn flakes, flatten and bake on a greased tray at 350°F., 180°C., Gas Mark 4, until brown.

183 NEW ZEALAND FUDGE CAKE

(No oven baking)

1 lb. crushed biscuits.
1 tablespoon cocoa.
1 cup walnuts (chopped).
1 cup dates (chopped).
2 tablespoons honey or golden syrup.
1 egg.
Some marmalade and/or mixed peel.
Vanilla to taste.
Icing as desired.
¼ lb. butter.

Dissolve over heat the honey/golden syrup, butter, beaten egg.
Cool, and add vanilla to taste.
Put the dry ingredients into a bowl, pour the dissolved mixture over them and mix well.
Butter a shallow tin and press the mixture well down into it.
Ice.
When quite cold and set this cake can be cut into fingers and is delicious on its own or eaten with bread and butter.

184 PARKIN

1 lb. fine oatmeal.
½ lb. flour.
½ lb. demerara sugar.
1 lb. treacle.
½ lb. butter.
2 teaspoons baking powder.
2 teaspoons ground ginger.
1 teaspoon allspice.
1 teaspoon salt.
1 teaspoon bicarbonate of soda dissolved in ½ cup milk.

The butter is placed in a dish in the oven to melt, along with the treacle, whilst the other ingredients are placed in a bowl.
Bake 1½ to 2 hours.
The mixture will rise to the top of the tin whilst in the oven, but sinks down in the middle when it is cooked. It must be *kept* for some time to get soft, and then the paper easily peels off it.
This makes two good-sized ones.

185 RASPBERRY BUNS

8 ozs. flour.
1 level teaspoon baking powder.
A pinch of salt.
3 ozs. sugar.
2½ ozs. margarine.
Milk to mix.
Raspberry jam.

Make a dough, roll out on floured board, cut into rounds with medium cutter, about ⅜ of an inch thick.
Put a teaspoonful of jam in the centre, gather up damped edges, and place on greased tin, smooth side up.
Cook in moderate oven till pale brown.

186 PRINCESS SPONGE CAKE

To make sponge without eggs, take a cupful of caster sugar and of milk, two cups of plain flour and two level teaspoons baking powder.
Beat together thoroughly and bake in a moderate oven.
This can be in one cake tin or two sponge tins. Useful for trifles or fruit dishes.

187 SCRIPTURE CAKE

4½ cups flour.
1½ cups butter.
2 cups sugar.
2 cups raisins.
2 cups figs or sultanas.
1 cup chopped almonds.
½ cup milk.
2 teaspoons honey.
Spice to taste.
6 eggs.
A pinch of salt.
2 tablespoons baking powder.

Cream the butter and sugar.
Add eggs one by one.
Wash fruit, chop almonds.
Add flour, baking powder and salt gradually to the mixture.
Also put fruit, honey, spice and milk.
Mix well in a well-lined tin and bake for 2½ to 3 hours.

188 SEED LOAF

4 ozs. margarine or butter.
4 level tablespoons sugar.
2 eggs.
4 heaped tablespoons flour.

Cream sugar and margarine.
Add 2 eggs, then the flour.
Beat well.
Mix in a small teaspoonful of caraway seeds, or more according to taste.
Bake in a moderate oven.

189 SIMNEL CAKE

6 ozs. softened butter or block margarine.
3 whole eggs.
8 ozs. plain flour.
½ level teaspoon ground cinnamon.
4 ozs. glacé cherries, washed, dried and cut into quarters.
2 ozs. cut mixed peel, chopped.
4 ozs. sultanas.
Milk if necessary.
6 ozs. caster sugar.
1 egg white.
Pinch of salt.
½ level teaspoon nutmeg.
9 ozs. currants.
Finely grated rind of 1 lemon.
1 lb. almond paste.

Grease and line a 7-inch round cake tin with greased greaseproof paper. Cream the butter and sugar until pale and fluffy.
Lightly whisk the whole eggs and gradually beat into creamed mixture.
Sift the flour, salt and spices over the mixture and fold in with a metal spoon.
Add all the fruit and lemon rind, folding together to give a smooth dropping consistency. If too firm add a little milk.

Divide the almond paste in half. Lightly dust a surface with icing sugar and roll out one half to a 6½-inch circle.
Spoon half cake mixture into tin. Place round of almond paste on top, cover with remaining cake mixture. Level the surface gently with the back of a spoon.

Tie double thickness brown paper round the tin. Bake at 150°C. (300°F., Gas Mark 2) for about 2½ hours. When cooked the cake should be a rich brown colour, and firm to the touch. Cool in tin for about an hour, then turn out. Ease off the greaseproof paper and cool completely on a wire rack.
Divide remaining almond paste in two. Roll out one half to a 7½ inch circle and the rest into eleven small balls. Brush the lightly beaten egg white over the top of the cake and place the circle on top.
Crimp the edges and fix the balls round the top edge of the cake with a little of the egg white. Brush almond paste with remaining egg white and grill for a few minutes until the paste is well browned. Decorate as desired.

190 SHORTBREAD

8 ozs. butter.
8 ozs. flour.
3 ozs. ground rice.
4 ozs. caster sugar.
A pinch of salt.

Sieve the ground rice, salt and flour together.
Rub butter into the flour mixture and add sugar.
Knead until you have a paste and then place in a shallow pastry tin or round sponge tin.
Crimp the edges with the handle of a knife, prick all over.
Mark into sections (if liked) with a knife.
Bake for about 35 minutes at 350°F., 180°C., Gas Mark 4 until a pale golden colour.
Cool, and dust with caster sugar.

191 TREACLE FRUIT CAKE (MOIST)

1 lb. flour.
½ lb. margarine.
¼ lb. sugar.
¼ lb. treacle or golden syrup.
Flat teaspoon bicarbonate of soda.
6 ozs. currants.
6 ozs. sultanas.
2 ozs. chopped peel.
2 eggs.
1 gill milk.

Grease a large cake tin.
Beat fat and sugar.
Add syrup and tablespoon boiling water and pinch of salt.
Add eggs.
Add flour and fruit and milk.
Bake in a moderate oven 1½ hours.

192 BOILED FRUIT CAKE

½ pint strained strong tea.
5 ozs. butter.
6 ozs. soft brown sugar.
1 lb. mixed fruit.
2 teaspoons mixed peel.
1 lb. plain flour.
2 teaspoons bicarbonate of soda.
2 tablespoons malt vinegar.
2 tablespoons orange juice.

Put tea in saucepan with fat, sugar and fruit.
Boil and then simmer till fat melts. Cool.
Sieve flour and bicarb., add to mixture with vinegar and orange juice.
Put into two lined cake tins (8-inch).
Bake 150°C., 300°F., Gas Mark 2, for 30 minutes, then reduce to a slow oven for 1½ hours.
Test with skewer.
Store 2–3 days before cutting.

193 VICTORIA SPONGE

4 ozs. sugar.
4 ozs. margarine. } cream together 15 minutes.
4 ozs. self-raising flour.
2 eggs. } add alternately to above, sifted flour and beaten eggs.

Bake in oven 365°F., 185°C., Gas Mark 4.

194 VINEGAR CAKE

1 lb. flour.
½ lb. margarine and/or lard.
½ lb. sugar.
½ lb. dried fruit.
1 teaspoon mixed spice.
½ teaspoon bicarbonate of soda
1 teacup milk.
2 tablespoons vinegar.

Mix all dry ingredients.
Add soda and vinegar to milk and stir quickly into flour, etc.
Bake in a moderate oven for about 2 hours.

195 WARTIME CAKE

¼ lb. rolled oats.
¼ lb. margarine.
2 ozs. caster sugar (*or* granulated).

Beat margarine and sugar to a cream, mix in oats lightly.
Bake in a slow oven until golden brown.
Cut in fingers or keep whole.
Very good.

196 WALNUT SLICES

8 ozs. S.R. flour.
4 ozs. margarine.
2 ozs. caster sugar.
1 egg yolk.

Topping:
1 egg white.
4 ozs. icing sugar.
2 ozs. chopped walnuts.
apricot jam.

Rub fat into flour, add sugar and mix.
Bind together with egg yolk and press into greased swiss roll tin.
Spread lightly with jam.
Lightly whisk egg white (keep runny), fold in sifted icing sugar.
Add walnuts (reserve a few for the top).
Spread mixture over jam, sprinkle remaining walnuts over the top.
Bake till firm 350°F., 180°C., Gas Mark 4, approximately 30 minutes.
Cut into fingers while warm.

197 ANZACS

¼ lb. margarine.
3 teaspoons syrup.
¾ teacup sugar.
1 teaspoon bicarbonate of soda.
¾ teacup flour.
1 teacup oats.
1 teaspoon desiccated coconut.
1 teacup chopped walnuts.
2 tablespoons boiling water.

Warm margarine, syrup and sugar in pan.
Add soda dissolved in boiling water.
Add remaining ingredients, mix to moist consistency.
Put in small piles, leaving room for them to spread on cold baking trays which have been greased.
Bake in slow oven half an hour.

198 FATLESS SPONGE

3 eggs.
4 ozs. caster sugar.
3 ozs. plain flour.

Grease two 7-inch sandwich tins. Dust with mixture of flour and icing sugar.
Whisk eggs and sugar in a large bowl over hot water till thick, pale and creamy.
Remove from heat and whisk till cold.
If an electric whisk is used, no heat is necessary.
Fold in sieved flour using a metal spoon.
Pour the mixture into the tins and shake the tin gently to distribute the mixture evenly.
Bake 190°C., 375°F., Gas Mark 5, 20–25 minutes.

199 POTATO CAKE

1 lb. cooked mashed potato.
4 ozs. suet.
2 ozs. sultanas.
2 ozs. raisins.
1 oz. currants.
4 ozs sugar.
8 ozs. flour.

Mix potatoes and suet, add fruit and sugar, then flour.
Mix well, press into 8-inch sandwich sponge tin. Fork over top.
Bake middle of oven 350°F., 180°C., Gas Mark 4 for 45 minutes.
Best eaten while warm.

200 SOMERSET EASTER CAKES

Rub ½ lb. butter into ½ lb. plain flour.
Mix in 2 ozs. currants, ½ teaspoon mixed spice, ½ teaspoon cinnamon.
Add egg to make into dough firm enough to roll out.
Roll out ½ inch thick cut into rounds. Bake in moderate oven 20 minutes.

201 SCOTS MELODIES

4 ozs. rolled oats.
3 ozs margarine.
1 egg.
2 ozs sugar.
4 ozs. flour.
Grated rind of 1 orange.
1 teaspoon baking powder.
1 tablespoon golden syrup.
A little milk if needed.
Covering of chocolate.

Rub margarine into flour and oats. Add baking powder and sugar and orange rind.
Beat egg, add to warm syrup, add to oats, make paste. Roll out thinly, cut into shapes.
Bake in moderate oven. When cold sandwich with orange filling, coat with chocolate.

SCONES AND BREAD, ETC.

202 *BREAD BAPS*

(Quick rise)

1 lb. flour (warmed).
1 oz. yeast.
2 ozs. lard *or* cooking fat.
¼ oz. sugar.
1 teaspoon salt.
¼ pint milk.
¼ teacupful hot water.
2 to 3 tablespoons tepid water.

Sift flour and salt in a bowl.
Place yeast and sugar in small basin and cream together.
Add a little tepid water and leave to rise in a warm place.
Place fat in a basin and add 1 gill hot water, then when fat melts add cold milk.
Make a well in centre of flour, add yeast, then mix to a smooth dough with the tepid milk and fat.
Knead thoroughly.
Divide into 6 pieces.
Roll into a ball, then flatten like a thick tea-cake.
Place on floured baking sheet.
Rise ½ hour.
Bake 20 minutes 230°C., 450°F., Gas Mark 8.

203 *WHOLEMEAL BREAD*

3 lbs. wholemeal bread flour.
1 oz. lard.
1½ pints warm water.
1 oz. salt.
½ oz. caster sugar.
2 ozs. fresh yeast or 2 packets easy blend yeast.

Sieve the flour and salt into a bowl and rub in the lard. Mix fresh yeast with one teaspoon of the sugar and add to the lukewarm water (or put easy blend yeast in with the flour dry). Add

remaining sugar to dry ingredients.
Add to the flour and mix to a firm dough.
Knead for 10 minutes, put into a greased bowl, cover with damp cloth and leave for 1 hour to double in size.
Knead and then divide the dough into rolls or loaves. Cover and leave to prove about 20 to 30 minutes.
Bread will take about 40 minutes at 230°C., (450°F., Gas Mark 8). Rolls will take about 30 minutes at same temperature.

204 GIRDLE CAKES OR WELSH CAKES

8 ozs. self-raising flour.
3 ozs. granulated sugar.
4 ozs. margarine *or* butter.
3 ozs. currants.
A pinch of salt.
Milk.

Rub fat into flour, add sugar, salt and currants.
Mix to a stiff dough with a little milk.
Roll out not too thin.
Bake on hot girdle for 5 minutes each side.
Makes 18 cakes.

205 HAYSTACKS

12 ozs. wholemeal self-raising flour.
½ teaspoon baking powder.
Good pinch salt.
1 oz. butter or fat.
8 ozs. cheese.
2 teaspoons dried onion, crumbled small.
½ teaspoon dried mixed herbs.
1 egg.
Water to mix.

Mix flour, baking powder and salt, and rub in fat.
Stir in onion, herbs and grated cheese.
Beat egg into a small cup of water and use to mix flour, etc. to a soft but not sticky dough.
Roll out on a floured board to an oblong about ⅝″ thick.
Cut into squares and bake at 230°C., 450°F., Gas Mark 8, for about 15 minutes.

206 MALT LOAF

1 lb. raisins.
2 tablespoons malt extract.
1 egg, beaten.
6 ozs. soft dark brown sugar.
½ pint cold tea.
12 ozs. self-raising flour.
Pinch of salt.

Place raisins, sugar, malt and tea in a bowl and stir well. Leave to soak overnight. The next day stir in the flour and egg and mix well.
Divide mixture into 2 x 1 lb. loaf tins which have been greased and the bottom lined. Smooth the tops.
Bake at 160°C., 325°F., Gas Mark 3, for 1 to 1¼ hours until firm to touch.
Cool on a wire rack.
If desired decorate with cherries.

207 POTATO CAKES

Work equal quantities of mashed potatoes and flour lightly together into a stiff paste with a little cream (*or* melted butter).
Add salt and a few sultanas *or* currants.
Cut into small rounds and cook on top of stove, not in oven.

208 DROP SCONES

4 ozs. plain flour.
¼ level teaspoon salt.
1 level teaspoon cream of tartar.
1 oz. caster sugar.
1 egg.
½ level teaspoon bicarbonate of soda.
¼ pint milk.
½ oz. margarine.

Sieve dry ingredients, stir in sugar.
Mix to thick batter with egg and milk.
Melt margarine, stir in. Batter should drop easily from spoon or pour from jug.
Makes approximately 12 scones.

209 OVEN SCONES

8 ozs. S.R. flour.
½ level teaspoon salt.
1 level teaspoon baking powder.
1–2 ozs margarine or butter.
¼ pint milk.
Beaten egg glaze (opt.)

Pre-heat baking sheet.
Sift flour, salt and baking powder together.
Rub in fat till it resembles fine breadcrumbs.
Make well in centre, add enough milk to make soft dough.
Turn onto lightly floured board, knead gently; pat out with the hand until ¾ inch thick.
Cut into 10–12 rounds using cutter dipped in flour, or cut into triangles with a knife.
Place on baking sheet, if liked, glaze with milk or egg.
Bake top of the oven 230°C., 450°F., Gas Mark 8; 8–10 minutes.
Cool on rack, serve split and buttered.

Fruit scones: Add 2 ozs. either currants, raisins, sultanas or mixture of fruit to the above ingredients.

210 CHEESE SCONES

8 ozs. S.R. flour.
1½ ozs. butter or margarine.
1 level teaspoon dry mustard.
3–4 ozs. mature cheddar cheese, grated.
Salt.
¼ pint milk.
1 level teaspoon baking powder.

Grease baking tray. Sift flour, baking powder and salt together.
Rub in fat until resembles fine breadcrumbs.
Stir in half the cheese, mustard and enough milk to give soft dough.
Roll out or pat out to ¾-inch thick and cut into rounds with 2-inch plain cutter.
Place on baking tray, brush tops with milk and sprinkle with remaining cheese.
Bake 220°C., 425°F., Gas Mark 7. 10 minutes.

211 WHITE BREAD

3 lbs. strong plain flour.
1 oz. lard.
1 teaspoon sugar.
1 oz. salt.
1 oz. fresh yeast or 2 packets of easy blend yeast.
1½ pints warm water.

Sieve the flour and salt into a bowl and rub in the lard. Mix fresh yeast with sugar and add to the lukewarm water (or put easy blend yeast with the flour dry).

Add to the flour and mix to a firm dough. Knead for 10 minutes. Put into a greased bowl, cover with damp cloth and leave for 1 hour to double in size.

Knead and then divide the dough into rolls or loaves. Cover and leave to prove about 20 minutes.

Bread will take about 40 minutes at 230°C. (450°F, Gas Mark 8). Rolls will take about 20 minutes at same temperature.

212 BANANA AND WALNUT TEABREAD

7 ozs. S.R. flour (sifted).
½ level teaspoon salt.
¼ teaspoon bicarbonate of soda.
6 ozs. sugar.
3 ozs. butter
2 beaten eggs..
1 lb. mashed bananas.
4 ozs. chopped walnuts.

Grease and line oblong 1 lb. loaf tin.

Sift flour, salt, bicarb.

Cream butter, sugar until pale and fluffy. Add egg a little at a time.

Add bananas, beat in well; add flour and nuts.

Put into tin, bake 180°C., 350°F., Gas Mark 4, 1¼ hours until firm and well risen.

Turn out onto rack to cool. Keep for 24 hours before eating, serve sliced with butter.

213 FRUIT LOAF WITHOUT SUGAR

8 ozs. plain wholemeal flour and 1 level teaspoon baking powder
1 lb. dried fruit (mixed).
½ pint tea
1 beaten egg.
(or 8 ozs. S.R. wholemeal flour, or 4 ozs. wholemeal flour and 4 ozs. white flour, using baking powder if plain flour).

Put 8 ozs. fruit and ¼ pint tea in liquidizer and blend for a minute or two.
Add to the rest of the fruit and tea in a basin and leave overnight to release the natural sugar in the fruit.
Next day, add beaten egg and flour. Mix well.
Bake in a 2 lb. loaf tin for 1¼-1½ hours at 160°C., 325°F., Gas Mark 3.
Best eaten sliced with butter.

214 HONEY NUT BREAD

6 ozs. plain white flour.
6 ozs. plain wholemeal flour.
4 teaspoons baking powder.
6 tablespoons melted butter.
12 fluid ozs milk.
4 ozs chopped walnuts.
1 beaten egg.
6 ozs. honey

Sift flours and baking powder.
Mix in honey, nuts, egg, butter and milk.
Combine, do not overstir.
Pour into oiled 2 lb. loaf tin. Bake at 180°C., 350°F., Gas Mark 4, for 50–60 minutes.
Slice and serve buttered.

215 TEA BREAD

In one cup of tea soak two cups of mixed dried fruit and one cup of brown sugar. Leave overnight. Next morning add one well beaten egg and two cups self-raising flour. Pour into greased loaf tin. Bake two hours, middle shelf, medium oven.

216 YORKSHIRE TEACAKES

1¾ lbs. plain flour.
¼ lb. lard.
2½ ozs. sugar.
½ teaspoon salt.
2 ozs. yeast.
2 ozs. currants.
2 ozs. sultanas.
Milk and water.

Rub fat into flour.
Cream yeast and pour into flour.
Stand in a warm place for 10 minutes.
Add fruit, mix to dough and knead until smooth.
Cover, and stand until risen.
Divide into cakes about 3 to 4 ozs. each.
Stand again until risen.
Bake in a hot oven, 450°F., 230°C., Gas Mark 8.

CHRISTMAS RECIPES

217 *CHRISTMAS CAKE*

(or Bride's Cake)

A large tin well lined:

- 12 ozs. self-raising flour.
- 8 ozs. butter.
- 8 ozs. caster sugar.
- 1½ lbs. currants.
- ¼ lb. mixed peel *or* cherries if preferred.
- ¼ teaspoon spice.
- 2 ozs ground almonds.
- 4 eggs.
- A medium-sized grated apple.
- A pinch of salt.

Beat fat and sugar and beat in eggs gradually with 1 oz. flour to 1 egg.

Stir in 4 ozs. flour and then stir in rest of the flour (4 ozs.) with fruit and spice and almonds and grated apple.

Mix well and bake for 3 hours in a steady oven.

This cake is fine in a dripping tin and keeps for months. It makes a good slab cake as a special treat.

218 *CHRISTMAS CAKE*

- 1 lb. 6 ozs. currants.
- 8 ozs. raisins.
- 4 ozs. mixed peel.
- 14 ozs. plain flour.
- ½ teaspoon cinnamon.
- 12 ozs. butter
- 6 eggs, beaten.
- 2–3 tablespoons of brandy or rum.
- 8 ozs. sultanas.
- 6 ozs. glacé cherries.
- 4 ozs. chopped almonds.
- Juice of ½ a lemon, and rind, grated.
- ½ teaspoon mace.
- 12 ozs. soft brown sugar.
- 1 tablespoon treacle.

Cream butter and sugar, then add alternately beaten eggs and flour, lemon and treacle. Mix in all other dry ingredients.

Put into lined tin (8-inch square or 9-inch round). Tie a thickness of brown paper around outside of tin. Bake at 130°C. (250°F., Gas Mark 4) for about 4 hours.

219 *ALMOND PASTE*

½ lb. ground almonds.
½ lb. caster sugar.
2 eggs.
About 2 drops almond essence.
½ lb. icing sugar.

Mix almonds and sugar.
Beat eggs and knead into nuts and add almond essence.
Spread on top of levelled cake, and smooth with a clean knife.

220 *CHRISTMAS PARTY TRIFLE*

6 small sponges.
¼ lb. macaroon biscuits.
3 ozs. ratafia biscuits.
2 ozs. chopped sweet almonds.
3 tablespoons raspberry jam.
¼ pint cream.
1 tablespoon caster sugar.
The whites of 3 eggs.
1 wineglassful raisin wine.

Cover bottom of dish with macaroons.
Slice sponge cakes and spread with jam.
Sprinkle over ratafia biscuits and soak with wine.
Make a pint of custard and pour over.
Sprinkle over the chopped almonds.
Beat up cream with sugar and then whites of eggs.
Mix them and heap lightly all over top of dish.
Decorate with crystallised fruits and silver balls.

221 *CHRISTMAS PUDDING*

1 lb. plain flour.
1 lb. suet.
1 lb. brown sugar.
1 lb. chopped mixed peel.
1 lb. currants.
1 teaspoonful mixed spice. } or to taste.
1 teaspoonful nutmeg. }
1½ lbs. raisins.
1½ lbs. sultanas.
1 lb. white breadcrumbs.
8 eggs – large.
5 – 6 fl. ozs. brandy or rum.

Mix and put into greased basins. Cover and boil for 8 hours. Reboil for 3 hours before serving.

222 *CHRISTMAS PUDDING WITHOUT EGGS*

½ lb. raisins.
½ lb. currants.
½ lb. sultanas.
½ lb. suet.
½ lb. finely chopped apples.
½ lb. demerara sugar.
¼ lb. mixed peel.
10 chopped almonds.
½ teaspoon mixed spice.
¼ lb. golden syrup *or* dark treacle.
¼ lb. grated breadcrumbs.
¼ lb. flour.
Grated rind and juice of ½ a lemon.
½ wineglass brandy or stout optional.)

Mix all ingredients except brandy or stout and allow to stand all night.
Stir well, add brandy or stout and steam for 6 hours.
Sufficient for 2 puddings. Will keep for a year if required.

223 *MINCEMEAT*

½ lb. raisins.
½ lb. sultanas.
½ lb. currants.
½ lb. sugar.
½ lb. chopped apples.
½ lb. suet (chopped finely).
¼ lb. mixed chopped peel.
2 teaspoons mixed spice.
Grated peel and juice of 1 lime (*or* orange).
1 gill of brandy or rum.

Stone raisins and wash sultanas and currants.
Mix all ingredients togther, and tie down in jars, and keep for a few weeks.
At *Christmas time,* fill pastry cases with mixture (mincemeat) and bake.
Serve with powdered sugar on top, and *brandy sauce.*

VEGETARIAN RECIPES

224 APPLE AND STILTON SAVOURY

6 ozs. Stilton.
¼ lb. cream cheese.
Salt and pepper.
4 medium dessert apples.
Vinaigrette dressing.
Lettuce leaves.

Rub Stilton through fine sieve. Mix in the cream cheese and seasoning.
Wash and polish the apples, cut a slice off the top of each.
Carefully scoop out the flesh, discard the cores, keep the rest.
Chop it up and toss in the vinaigrette dressing to prevent it discolouring.
Fill the apple shells with the cheese mixture.
Arrange on a bed of lettuce leaves surrounded with the chopped apple and serve extra vinaigrette.

225 CAULIFLOWER AND STILTON FLAN

1 medium cauliflower.
½ pint white sauce.
4 ozs. Stilton cheese.
7-inch flan ring lined with shortcrust pastry.

Cook cauliflower whole in boiling salted water.
Bake lined flan ring blind till just firm.
Sprinkle half the Stilton cheese in base of flan.
Place cooked cauliflower on top of cheese in one piece.
Cover with white sauce and sprinkle with remaining cheese.
Return to oven for 20 minutes to brown over and heat through.
Serve decorated with sprigs of parsley.

226 COLESLAW

2 cups shredded cabbage.
½ cup grated cucumber.
½ cup grated green pepper.
Salt and black pepper.
1 cup or more plain yoghurt.

Combine all ingredients and serve.

227 CUCUMBER WITH MUSHROOMS AND HERBS

1 large cucumber.
1½ ozs. butter.
1 small onion, diced.
1 teaspoon plain flour.
Grated nutmeg.
3 ozs. button mushrooms, sliced.
1 dessert spoon single cream or yoghurt.
1 dessert spoon white stock.
1 dessert spoon shredded sorrel.

Wash cucumber, dice, do not peel.
Cook till tender in enough salted water to cover.
Discard water, rinse cucumber and leave to drain. Melt butter in pan, braise onion over low heat, season.
Add mushrooms, braise till tender, return cucumber to pan, add cream and stock. Stir.
Stir in flour, bring to the boil gently, simmer 3 minutes.
Add sorrel (keep little for garnish) cook another minute.
Pour into warmed serving dish. Garnish with grated nutmeg and sorrel.

228 DODGERS

4 ozs. Irish cheddar cheese.
2 teaspoons baking powder.
1 tablespoon oatmeal.
¼ pint milk.
Fat or oil to fry.
1 oz. plain flour.
¼ teaspoon salt.
Black pepper.
½ teaspoon mixed herbs.

Cut cheese into small dice.
Sift flour, baking powder, salt; add oatmeal and pepper.
Add sufficient milk to make batter. Beat well, stir in cheese and herbs.
Heat a little oil or fat in a large non-stick pan, add batter one tablespoon at a time to make small fritters. Fry quickly on both sides. Drain well before serving.

229 HOT BLUE CHEESE AND CELERY MOUSSE

8 ozs. thinly sliced celery.
3 ozs. blue cheese.
4 egg whites.
Butter.
2 tablespoons single cream.
3 egg yolks.
Black pepper.
Browned breadcrumbs.

Cook celery in minimum of water for 30 minutes till really soft. Remove pan lid and boil till liquid evaporates.
Purée celery in blender with the cream and blue cheese. Cool.
Beat in egg yolks and pepper. Whisk egg whites till stiff, fold into mixture.
Turn into lightly buttered 2½ pint soufflé dish, cover with buttered foil.
Steam 30 minutes. Serve at once dusted with breadcrumbs.

230 OATIE SUPPER DISH

4 ozs. porridge oats.
2 ozs. cheese.
2 hardboiled eggs.
2 ozs. margarine.
1 onion.
3 to 4 tomatoes.
Salt and pepper.

Grease a pie dish well.
Put in a layer of sliced tomatoes, then a layer of chopped onion.
Add seasoning and moisten with a little milk or tomato juice.
Add sliced or halved eggs.
Rub the margarine into the oats till well mixed, add grated cheese and pinch of salt.
Spread on top of mixture and put a few thin pieces of margarine on top.
Bake in a moderate oven.

231 PARSLEY PIE

Chop parsley coarsley.
Mix with small pieces of butter, pepper and salt, and a beaten egg and milk to moisten.
Place in pie dish, or individual dishes, sprinkle with breadcrumbs and butter pieces.
Bake till cooked. Make slight hole, or holes for number of persons and break an egg into each. Bake till each egg is set.

232 POTATO AND LEEK PIE

Scrub and peel 2 lbs. potatoes. Cut into thick slices.
Wash 1 or 2 leeks and chop finely.
Mix 1 heaped tablespoon flour, 1 teaspoon salt, and pepper to taste.
Grease pie dish. Put in alternate layers of leek and potato, sprinkling with the seasoned flour. Top layer potatoes.
Put in 3 teacups of hot milk and bake in moderate oven for 1 hour.

233 ROMAN PIE

Boil 4 ozs. macaroni.
Butter a pie dish and put in half the macaroni.
Scald 4 or 5 tomatoes and skin.
Hard boil two eggs and slice.
Have 2 ozs. grated cheese, layer alternately with the macaroni, tomatoes, eggs and salt and pepper.
Add a little grated onion and 8 or 10 mushrooms (sliced). Repeat the layers, and end up with the tomatoes.
Cover the top thickly with breadcrumbs.
Put dessertspoonful butter in pan, stir in half teaspoon flour, same of made mustard; add half teacup of stock, blend well, stir till it boils, pour over the mixture.

234 ONION CREAM TART

6 ozs. rich short crust pastry.
1 oz. butter.
1 clove garlic.
4 tablespoons double cream.
12 anchovy fillets.
1½ lbs. onions.
2 tablespoons oil.
1 egg plus 1 egg yolk.
Salt, pepper.
12 stoned green olives.

Make up pastry, leave to rest.
Slice onions finely, add to heated butter and oil in pan. Cook very slowly with lid on till soft and tender.
Add crushed garlic half way through cooking which may take up to one hour.
Line buttered 7 inch deep flan tin with pastry. Prick the bottom with a fork.
Remove onions from the heat, beat in the eggs with the cream, add seasoning.
Pour into flan case. Arrange anchovies in a criss cross pattern over the top.
Fill in with the olives.
Bake 200°C., 400°F., Gas Mark 6, for 30 minutes.

235 SAVOURY PANCAKES

½ pint pancake batter.
½ oz. butter.
1½ lbs. tomatoes.
1 clove garlic.
Salt, pepper.
½ lb. cream cheese.
1 onion.
1 tablespoon oil.
1 teaspoon chopped parsley.
2 basil leaves or ¼ teaspoon dried basil.
1 lb. spinach.

Make up pancake batter, leave to stand for up to 2 hours.
Chop onion, soften in heated butter and oil till transparent, add skinned, chopped tomatoes, chopped herbs and seasoning; simmer 20 minutes.
Rub through sieve; keep sauce warm.
Wash and strip spinach, cook without water for 5 minutes till tender.
Drain well, season. Add cream cheese and blend. Reheat gently.
Make 8 medium sized pancakes; put 2 spoonfuls of mixture in centre of each. Roll up.
Arrange pancakes on heated serving dish; pour over hot tomato sauce; sprinkle with chopped parsley and serve immediately.

236 SPINACH AND LENTIL ROULADE

6 ozs. lentils.
2 level tablespoons tomato ketchup.
4 ozs. butter.
1lb. trimmed spinach.
½ pint milk.
Dry breadcrumbs.
1 small onion, finely chopped.
1 level teaspoon creamed horseradish.
Salt and pepper.
2 ozs. flour.
2 eggs, separated.

Butter and line 11-inch swiss roll tin.
Cook lentils with onion in large pan of boiling salted water. Drain well, return to pan, heat to evaporate excess moisture.
Add ketchup and horseradish, plus 2 ozs. butter. Put through sieve or purée in a blender. Season and set aside.
Cook spinach gently, sprinkled with salt, for 3–4 minutes. Turn into colander, press out excess liquid; chop finely.
Make sauce: Melt remaining butter, add flour, cook gently, stirring 1 minute. Take off heat, gradually add milk; bring to boil, cook till thickens. Remove from heat, stir in spinach and egg yolks, season.
Whisk egg whites till stiff, gently fold in to spinach mixture. Bake in prepared tin for 20 minutes in a medium oven till well risen and golden.
Turn out on to greased paper sprinkled with breadcrumbs, peel off paper.
Spread lentil mixture over surface, roll up swiss roll style; return to oven 5 minutes. Serves four.

237 STUFFED AUBERGINES AU GRATIN

2 large or 4 small aubergines.
2½ ozs. butter.
¼ lb. chopped onion.
1 large clove garlic.
Good pinch sweet basil.
Pepper.
¼ pint Bechamel sauce.
2 tablespoons fresh breadcrumbs.
Salt.
2 ozs. olive oil.
¼ lb. mushrooms.
1 bay leaf.
1 teaspoon finely chopped parsley.
4 large skinned tomatoes.
2 tablespoons grated Gruyere, Parmesan or strong Cheddar.

Cut aubergines in half lengthways; without damaging skins, make cuts across the exposed surfaces.
Sprinkle with salt and leave till drops of moisture appear.
Heat 2 ozs. butter and oil in pan.
Pat the aubergines dry, cook them gently, cut side down, until the skins go brown.
Remove from pan, add chopped onion; add more oil if needed, cook quickly but do not brown. When partly cooked add chopped mushrooms, garlic, herbs, salt and pepper.
Mix together, cook 5 minues, add tomatoes (chopped).
Meanwhile scoop out middle from aubergines and add to the vegetables, remove the bay leaf and season.
If the stuffing is too moist add a little breadcrumbs or cooked rice.
Fill the shells with the mixture and place in an ovenproof dish.
Coat each one lightly with the bechamel sauce to which has been added 2 tablespoons of the cheese.
Fry the rest of the breadcrumbs in ½ oz. butter, mix with grated cheese and sprinkle over the top of the dish.
Bake in hot oven to brown the gratin.

238 VEGETABLE PÂTÉ

4 ozs. butter.
2 sticks celery.
2 level teaspoons lemon rind.
6 tablespoons cream.
1–2 garlic cloves.
Salt, pepper.
1 medium onion finely chopped.
2 level tablespoons flour.
1 tablespoon lemon juice.
3 slices bread.
8 ozs. mushrooms.
Cocktail gherkins.

Heat butter gently in pan, add onion and crushed garlic, cook without colouring, 5 minutes.
Toss chopped celery and flour together, add to pan with chopped mushrooms. Cook 5–10 minutes.
Add pepper to taste, cool. Add lemon juice and rind and salt.
Mash all ingredients till smooth, add cream.
Spoon pâté into 4–6 ramekin dishes, smooth top. Cover, chill overnight.
Before serving, cut bread the same size as ramekin with pastry cutter, toast lightly, turn out pâté on to toast and decorate with sliced gherkin.

239 *YORKSHIRE APPLE CAKE*

- 12 ozs. shortcrust pastry.
- 2 ozs. grated Wensleydale cheese.
- 4 cooking apples, sliced.
- 3 ozs. caster sugar.

Line swiss roll tin with half the pastry.
Layer apples, cheese and sugar over.
Roll over remaining pastry to form a lid. Pinch edges together and seal.
Brush top with water, sprinkle with sugar.
Cook in medium oven, serve warm cut in slices.

MICROWAVE RECIPES

(600 watts)

240 QUICK KIPPER PÂTÉ

8 ozs. kipper fillets.
Salt and pepper.
1 teaspoon lemon juice.
1 teaspoon tomato purée.
5 ozs. double cream, whipped.

Place the kippers on a plate, cover with pierced microwave film and microwave on HIGH for 2–3 minutes.
Skin and flake the fish. Cool.
Mix the fish with the remaining ingredients.
Serve on French bread or toast.

241 PAPRIKA LIVER

¾ oz. butter.
Salt and pepper.
12 ozs. lamb's liver, well dried.
5 oz. carton soured cream.
1 level teaspoon paprika.

Heat the browning dish in the oven for 4 minutes.
Place the butter and seasoning into the dish; heat for a further 30 seconds.
Press the liver firmly on to the surface of the dish, turn over and repeat.
Cook the liver in the dish for 2½ minutes; turn the liver over and cook for a further 2½ minutes.
Remove the liver from the dish and stand it to one side.
Add the soured cream and paprika to the dish, mix well and cook for 2 minutes.
Pour the sauce over the liver and serve with noodles or rice.

242 MEATBALLS IN TOMATO SAUCE

1 lb. lean minced beef.
1 oz. fresh wholemeal breadcrumbs.
1 level teaspoon finely chopped onion.
1 oz. finely chopped green pepper.
1 oz. grated Parmesan.
Salt and Pepper.
1 egg, beaten.

Sauce:

15 oz. tin chopped tomato.
Salt and pepper.
1 level teaspoon chopped parsley (or ½ teaspoon basil).

Mix together the minced beef, breadcrumbs, onion, green pepper, cheese and seasoning. Bind together with the beaten egg.
Shape the mixture into 20 small meatballs and place them in a large casserole.
Cover and microwave on HIGH for 5–7 minutes, turning the meatballs after 3 minutes.
Combine the sauce ingredients, and pour over the meatballs.
Cover and microwave on HIGH for 8–10 minutes, or until the meatballs are cooked. Stir gently after every 4 minutes.
Serve with boiled brown rice. Serves 4.

243 CAULIFLOWER CHEESE

12 ozs. frozen or fresh cauliflower florets.
1 oz. margarine.
1 oz. flour.
Seasoning.
½ pint milk.
2 ozs. grated cheese.

Microwave cauliflower in bag for 4 minutes.
Meanwhile, blend all the sauce ingredients except grated cheese until smooth.
Remove cauliflower from microwave and cook sauce for approximately 3 minutes, stirring occasionally until sauce thickens.
Add grated cheese and use to cover cooked cauliflower.
Garnish and serve.

244 CRÈME CARAMEL

Caramel:	2 tablespoons granulated sugar. 2 tablespoons water.
Egg Custard:	½ pint milk. 1 tablespoon sugar. 2 eggs.

Caramel:

Stir the sugar and water in a large heatproof jug and microwave on HIGH, stirring once only, until sugar is dissolved – approximately 1 minute.

Caramelize the sugar syrup by bringing to the boil. Cook approximately 3–4 minutes. Inspect every half-minute as the syrup burns quickly.

Pour into the base of a 1-pint ovenproof soufflé dish.

Custard:

Beat the eggs and sugar, add the milk. Beat well and strain over the caramel. Cook, turning once, approximately 3½–4 minutes.

Note: Be very careful when preparing the caramel as sugar syrup is very hot.

245 WHOLEWHEAT LOAF

1 level teaspoon caster sugar.
1 sachet dried powdered yeast.
Approx. ¾ pint warm water.
1½ lbs. wholewheat flour.
¾ level teaspoon salt.
1 oz. margarine.

Sieve together the flour, salt, sugar and yeast.

Melt the margarine in the warm water, stir into the flour mixture. If the mixture is too dry add a little more water.

Knead the dough until smooth in texture. It should not be sticky.

Place in a greased container. Cover with a polythene bag or microwave film, and leave until doubled in size.

Remove cover and microwave on HIGH for 6–8 minutes or until the loaf is cooked through. If the cooker has no turntable the dish should be rotated every 2 minutes.

Turn out of the container and if liked, brown under a pre-heated grill.

246 CHRISTMAS PUDDING

1½ ozs. plain flour.
¼ level teaspoon nutmeg.
½ level teaspoon mixed spice.
Pinch ground cloves.
1½ ozs. fresh white breadcrumbs.
2 ozs. soft brown sugar.
2 ozs shredded suet.
10 ozs. mixed dried fruit.
Grated rind of 1 orange and 1 lemon.
1 egg.
1 dessertspoon black treacle.
⅛ pint Guinness or dark beer.
1 tablespoon brandy (optional).

Sift flour and spices into a bowl, add breadcrumbs, sugar, suet, flour and orange and lemon rind.
Mix thoroughly.
Add egg, treacle, beer and brandy – stir briskly.
Place in a 1-pint basin and cover with microwave film – make slits in covering to prevent 'ballooning'.
Cook pudding for 5–6 minutes. Allow to 'rest' for 5 minutes before turning out.

247 SPONGE PUDDING

4 ozs. S.R. flour.
pinch salt.
2 large eggs.
4 ozs. soft margarine.
4 ozs. soft dark brown sugar.
2 teaspoons golden syrup.
½ teaspoon vanilla essence.
2 tablespoons cold milk.
3 tablespoons golden syrup.
2-pint pudding basin, greased.

Sift the flour and salt together. Beat the eggs separately.
Beat the margarine and sugar together until really fluffy.
Stir in the syrup and vanilla essence.
Beat in the eggs gradually, then fold in the flour.
Stir in the milk. The mixture should be a rather wet batter and of a dark brown colour.
Spoon the 2 tablespoons of syrup into the base of the prepared bowl and pour the batter on top. Cover the bowl loosely with microwave film, sealing it at the sides.
Microwave on HIGH for 4–7 minutes until the pudding is *just* dry on top and shrinks away from the sides of the basin.

248 CHOCOLATE TOPS

2 ozs. S.R. flour.
½ oz. cocoa powder.
2 ozs. caster sugar.
2 ozs. margarine.
1 egg.
2 ozs. block chocolate (melted for topping).

Cream together flour, cocoa, sugar, margarine and egg. Put a teaspoon of the mixture into paper cake cases. Microwave for 1½ minutes.
Allow to cool and top with melted chocolate.

249 BANANA AND ORANGE TEABREAD

10 ozs. self-raising flour.
2 ozs. bran buds.
4 ozs. dark brown sugar.
2 ozs. margarine, softened.
3 drops gravy browning.
½ teaspoon salt.
1 tablespoon milk.
2 medium bananas, mashed.
1 large egg.
Grated rind and juice of an orange.

Line a loaf dish with kitchen paper.
Mix all ingredients in a bowl.
Place into the loaf dish and level out.
Cook on MEDIUM power for 11 minutes.
Turn out immediately. Leave to cool and serve sliced with butter.
N.B. This loaf improves with keeping.

250 RUBY PEARS

Cooking container—2½ pint casserole.
Cooking time—9 minutes.
Number of servings—4

4 well-shaped pears, peeled.
5 fl. ozs. water.
5 ozs. sugar.
Red food colouring.
1 lemon (juice and grated rind).
4 cloves.

Heat water and sugar for about (a) 4 minutes. Stir to ensure that the sugar is dissolved.
Add pears, lemon juice lemon rind and cloves and cook for (b) 5 minutes.
Spoon the syrup over the pears once during cooking. Carefully remove the pears.
Add red colouring to syrup for a bright red effect.
Return pears to syrup and turn frequently for an even colour.
Serve hot or cold with cream.

500 watt: (a) 5 minutes (b) 5½–6 minutes
650 watt: (a) PL9 4 minutes (b) PL9 4 minutes

251 COQ AU VIN

Cooking time—1 hour.
Cooking container—4 pint casserole.
Number of servings—4–5.

- 3 lbs. jointed chicken.
- 1 oz. butter.
- 1 tablespoon oil.
- 2 rashers bacon cut into small pieces.
- ½ pint red wine.
- 1 large onion, sliced.
- Salt and pepper..
- 4 ozs. button mushrooms..
- Bayleaf.
- Mixed herbs.

Heat the oil and butter in a frying pan. Fry the chicken joints till golden brown, place in the casserole with all the other ingredients. Cook covered for (a) 50 minutes.
Stir every 20 minutes.

500 watt: (a) 1¼ hours
650 watt: (a) PL6 1 hour.

JAMS, ETC.

252 *APPLE LEMON CURD*

½ lb. apples.
½ lb. sugar.
Rind and juice of 2 small lemons.
2 ozs. butter.
2 eggs.

Boil and pulp the apples and grate the lemon rind.
Add juice and rinds to the apples, add sugar and eggs, and mix thoroughly.
Put all in a saucepan in which the butter has been melted.
Stir over heat for ½ an hour.

253 *APRICOT JAM*

1 lb. dried apricots.
Pour over them 3 pints of boiling water.
Stand for 24 hours.
Boil until tender, then add 2 lbs. sugar and 1 oz. almonds (if liked), cut into pieces.
Boil until it sets—stir constantly.

254 *APPLE AND APRICOT JAM*

4 lbs. apples.
1 lb. apricots.
6 lbs. sugar.
3 pints water.

Wash apricots, cut into pieces and soak for 24 hours.
Grease pan.
Peel and cut up apples into small pieces.
Put apples, apricots and juice from apricots into pan and simmer until tender.
Add the sugar and allow to dissolve slowly.
Bring to the boil and boil for 20 minutes or until set, when tested.
Pour into warm jars and cover.

255 BLACKBERRY JAM

4 lbs. blackberries.
4 lbs. sugar.
2 tablespoons lemon juice.
½ pint water.

Grease the pan to prevent sticking.
Wash berries in slightly salted water.
Put the berries, water and lemon juice in the pan and simmer until the berries are soft.
Add sugar and allow to dissolve slowly.
Bring to the boil and boil rapidly, stirring occasionally, for 10 minutes. Test for setting after 10 minutes, boil longer if necessary.
Pour into warm jars and cover.

256 ELDERBERRY JELLY

Stalk the fruit, put into a jar and stand in a pan of boiling water, or a hot oven.
Cook gently.
Strain through a jelly bag, and to every pint of juice allow 1 lb. sugar.

257 GREEN GOOSEBERRY JAM

2 quarts gooseberries.
Add 1 quart water and bring slowly to the boil.
Mash them and cook them for 20 minutes.
Add 6 lbs. sugar, and after jam has come to the boil again, boil for 5 minutes only.
Let it cool slightly before putting into jars.
If cooked in a copper preserving pan this jam will keep its green colour.

258 LEMON CURD

2 lbs. loaf sugar.
½ lb. butter *or* margarine.
Rind and juice of 4 lemons.

Put fat and sugar in thick saucepan.
Squeeze lemons and pour over fat and sugar.
Add grated rinds.
Place pan over low heat and melt contents to a clear syrup.
Stand aside to cool.
Beat the eggs well and add to the cool syrup.
Return pan to low heat and stir constantly until the whole just comes to the boil and thickens.
Pour into warm jars.

259 *MARMALADE*

2 lbs. cut fruit (Seville oranges and 1 lemon).
6 pints water.
6 lbs. sugar.

Quarter and peel the fruit.
Remove some of the thickest peel and place in a large cup.
Removing any thick pith, cut up fruit in small pieces.
Put pips in cup with pith—tie all in muslin.
In preserving pan place: Peel, cut finely.
Fruit pulp.
Water.
Pip and pith bag.

Bring to boil (evening).
Cover with greaseproof paper and lid.
Place in slow oven overnight.

Next morning:
Boil without lid for 20 minutes.
Well squeeze out pip bag (between 2 saucers same way up) and remove.
Add sugar (not necessary to heat it).
Boil till it jells (40 minutes or less).

260 *MEDLAR JAM*

4lbs. medlars.
4 lemons.
3 pints water.

Simmer fruit until tender, then pass through a sieve.
Add ¾ lb. white sugar to each pound of fruit, return to pan and boil rapidly until set.

261 ORANGE MARMALADE

2 lbs. Seville oranges.
1 lb. fruit (1 lemon, 2 sweet oranges).
6 pints water.
6 lbs sugar.

Cut oranges and squeeze, saving juice in pan. Cut peel into quarters and scrape pith into bowl with pips. Then slice thinly and add to juice, and water.

Put pips and pith into muslin bag and add to rest of ingredients. Cook slowly for about 2 hours until cooked, then add sugar and bring to boil (about 30 minutes). Have cold saucers ready and test a teaspoonful which when cold should set. Leave for a while, then pot and cover in the usual way.

262 PEACH JAM

When ripe pare the fruit as thin as possible and weigh them.

Lay them in halves on a dish the hollow side upwards, and strew over them an equal weight of finely powdered sugar.

Break the stones and blanch the kernels.

After the fruit has laid twelve hours, pour it, with the sugar, juice and kernels into a preserving pan.

Let it simmer very gently until clear—the scum *must* be taken off as it rises.

Take the pieces out singly, put them into pots, and pour the syrup and kernels over them.

263 RHUBARB AND ORANGE JAM

Chip off in very thin bits the skin of 6 sweet oranges (a razor is excellent for this).

Take off the white pith and remove the pips.

Add the pulp to the cut peel.

To every 6 oranges, add 1½ quarts of rhubarb cut very small and measured in a quart measure.

Mix together and to 1 lb. fruit allow 1 lb. sugar.

Boil in the normal way.

264 SLOE JELLY

Wash half-ripe sloes.
Put in a pan, cover with water and boil until pulped, with a few crab apples.
When ready strain through a jelly bag, and let it drip.
To each pint of juice allow ¾ lb. sugar.
Boil until it jells.
Pour into small jars and seal, keeping it dark and dry.

265 STRAWBERRY JAM

6 lbs. strawberries.
7 lbs. preserving sugar.

Boil berries with 3 lbs. sugar for 20 minutes.
Add remainder of sugar (previously warmed) and boil rapidly until set.
This jam will not fail to thicken.

CHUTNEYS AND PICKLES

266 APPLE CHUTNEY

3 lbs. sour apples.
1½ lbs. brown sugar.
1 lb. seedless raisins.
2 lbs. onions.
1 dessertspoonful ginger.
2 lemons.
1 tablespoon mustard seed.
Pepper and salt.
1 quart malt vinegar.

Peel the apples and onions, and mince them with the raisins.
Put this mixture into a saucepan, and add the grated rind and strained juice of the lemons and all the other ingredients.
Bring to the boil and simmer gently until tender, stirring frequently.
Allow to cool before sealing down, and keep for 6 weeks before using.
Very good.

267 APPLE AND GREEN TOMATO CHUTNEY

2 lbs. apples.
1½ lbs. tomatoes.
1 lb. onions.
1½ lbs. brown sugar.
A little garlic.
12 chillies.
1 dessertspoon ginger.
1 dessertspoon salt.
1 saltspoon cayenne pepper.
½ lb. sultanas.
1 pint vinegar.

Mince all ingredients, add vinegar, stand all night, and boil 3 hours.

268 DAMSON PICKLE

2 quarts damsons.
1½ pints vinegar.
2 lbs. loaf sugar.

Prick the damsons all over.
Sprinkle with the sugar (crushed) and let them stand for 24 hours.
Pour the syrup from them into a saucepan—add vinegar and a few cloves.
Bring to boil and pour the boiling vinegar mixture over the damsons.
Let them stand another 24 hours, after which give them a gentle simmer for about ½ hour.
The fruit remains whole in a deliciously spicy syrup.
When cool put into glass jars and store.

269 THREE-FRUIT CHUTNEY

2 lbs. marrow.
2 lbs. apples, weighed after peeling.
½ lb. dried apricots.
1½ lbs. demerara sugar.
3 ozs. preserving ginger, shredded.
½ oz. white mustard seed.
¾ oz. salt.
1 teaspoon turmeric.
2 teaspoons cornflour.
½ teaspoon garlic chopped very fine, or garlic powder.
½ teaspoon cayenne pepper.
1 pint vinegar.
Vinegar and water to cover the apricots.

Wash the apricots and soak for 24 hours in vinegar and water.
Cut the marrow into cubes, strew with salt, leave overnight, then rinse well. If it is a tough marrow simmer till fairly tender and strain.
Next day, simmer the apples to a pulp, add the sugar and the other ingredients, viz:
(a) the apricots (cut up small) and their juice;
(b) the prepared marrow;
(c) the spices, etc. mixed to a smooth paste with the vinegar.
Simmer 30 – 40 minutes, till the marrow is tender, bottle and store.

270 GOOSEBERRY CHUTNEY

2 lbs. green gooseberries.
1 lb. dates.
2 lbs. brown sugar.
1 lb. raisins (stoned).
¼ lb. whole ginger.
1 head of garlic.
½ teaspoon cayenne pepper.
1 tablespoon salt.
2 pints malt vinegar.

Bruise ginger well and steep in the vinegar overnight.
Mince the rest of the ingredients and add to the strained vinegar.
Boil 1½ hours.
Bottle and seal when cold.
Makes eight 1 lb. jars.

271 DARTMOOR GOOSEBERRY MINT PRESERVE

(A very nice change from mint sauce or mint jelly)

1½ lbs. gooseberries.
1 lb. granulated sugar.
2 large bunches of mint.
About three parts of a ½ pint of white wine vinegar.

Gently cook the gooseberries until skins are very soft with the vinegar and 1 bunch of mint.
Take this mint out before adding the sugar; then, when the sugar has dissolved, add the second bunch of mint after bruising it.
Cook until thick enough for chutney.
(Note: This is best made when the gooseberry skins are still tender, it looks better and tastes nicer not overcooked, as green as possible. The two flavours go wonderfully well together and it keeps all its flavour for years, although the colour darkens somewhat with age in the second year. It is far less trouble than making mint jelly, and will go much further it wanted for a family).

272 HOT PICKLE

4 lbs. green tomatoes.
2 lbs. apples.
4 large onions.
2 quarts vinegar.
1 lb. brown sugar.
2 ozs. mustard seed.
Dessertspoon ground ginger.
½ teaspoon cayenne.
½ lb. raisins, chopped and stoned.

Prepare ingredients, slice tomatoes, apples and onions, sprinkle with salt and leave overnight.
Boil in an enamel pan until soft, gently simmering only.
Seal in pound jars.

273 JELLIED BEETROOT

3 or 4 medium-sized beetroot.
1 pineapple jelly (whole packet).
¼ pint vinegar (scant) }
¼ pint water (good) } making rather more than ½ pint liquid.

Boil beetroot in salted water until tender.
Cut into slices or cubes, as preferred.
Arrange in bowl or mould.
Dissolve jelly in vinegar and water heated almost to boiling point, and pour over the prepared beetroot.
Allow to set.
No other flavoured jelly gives the same result as pineapple.
This is an excellent addition to a green salad.

274 MARROW CHUTNEY

1 lb. marrow (you can use apple or rhubarb).
1 lb. onions.
1 lb. tomatoes.
¼ lb. sultanas.
½ lb. sugar.
3 chillies.
3 cloves.
1 tablespoon salt.
1 pinch mixed spice.
½ pint vinegar.

Cut up marrow in small cubes, sprinkle with salt, and allow to stand overnight.
Next day drain off the liquid, then add onions and tomatoes.
Cut both up small, add the vinegar and bring to the boil.
Add sugar and sultanas and the other ingredients and cook until tender, then cool and bottle when cold.

275 MINT JELLY

Cook 2 lbs. sour apples in ½ pint of vinegar.
Strain, and to each pint of juice allow 1 lb. sugar.
Boil for 10 minutes.
Add 1 tablespoon of chopped mint to each pint of juice.
Put in small pots and store in a cool place.

276 PICCALILLI

2 cauliflowers.
2 cucumbers.
2 lbs. shallots.
1 medium marrow.
1 quart vinegar.
1 oz. whole spice (all).
½ oz. ground ginger.
½ oz. turmeric (powder).
1 oz. mustard (powder).
1 tablespoon cornflour.
¼ lb. sugar (more if liked sweet).

Prepare vegetables and sprinkle with salt overnight; drain.
Boil most of vinegar, mix powders with the cold left, and add.
Add vegetables and boil for 15 minutes.

277 QUINCE AND LEMON CHUTNEY

1½ lbs. quinces.
½ lemon.
1 shallot.
1 clove garlic.
4 ozs. raisins.
2 ozs. chopped stem ginger.
1 lb. sugar (½ granulated, ½ Barbados).
½ teaspoonful each of:
ground cinnamon.
coriander.
black pepper.
salt.
¼ teaspoonful ground cloves.
½ pint white vinegar.

Peel and core the quinces.
Chop them with the shallots and lemon (pips removed).
Put all into a heavy pan with the raisins, ginger, spices and sugar.
Add the vinegar and bring the mixture to the boil.
Simmer slowly, stirring from time to time, until the fruit is cooked and the mixture is thick and looks like chutney.
It takes about ¾ hour.
Pot immediately.

278 RED TOMATO CHUTNEY

1½ pints vinegar.
1¾ lbs. tomatoes.
1¾ lbs. apples.
1½ lbs. demerara sugar.
½ lb. shallots.
6 ozs. sultanas.
1¾ ozs. salt.
A little ginger.

Place vinegar and sugar in enamel pan, stir over low heat till dissolved, bring to boil, remove scum.
Slice fruit and shallots and add to vinegar, add other ingredients and simmer until thick.
Peel tomatoes, if liked, dipping in boiling water for a few seconds.

279 RIPE TOMATO CHUTNEY

Boil 2 lbs. chopped sour apples till quite pulpy in 2 pints vinegar.
Meanwhile slice 2 lbs. peeled tomatoes.
Add these to the pulped apples, along with 6 ozs. chopped dried fruit, 1 lb. chopped onions, 2 lbs. chopped shallots, 1 lb. sugar, 1 oz. mustard seed, 1 oz. garlic, and a good dash of black pepper.
Boil gently for 1½ hours.
About 10 minutes before the chutney is cooked add a pinch of ginger and common salt to taste.
Bottle while hot and seal tightly.

280 RUNNER BEAN CHUTNEY

2 lbs. kidney beans (peeled and sliced).
4 to 5 onions.
1½ lbs. demerara sugar.
1½ tablespoons mustard.
1½ tablespoons cornflour.
1½ pints vinegar.
1½ tablespoons turmeric.

Peel and slice beans, cut onions up small.
Boil beans and onions in salt water (enough to cover them) until tender.
Strain and drain well, then cut up small, or better still put through the mincer.
Add the sugar and 1¼ pints of vinegar and boil for 15 minutes.
Mix turmeric, mustard and cornflour with the other ¼ pint vinegar and add to the beans, etc. and boil for another 15 minutes.
Allow to cool and put into jars.

281 SWEET APPLE CHUTNEY

4 lbs. prepared apples.
3 lbs. demerara sugar.
2 lbs. sultanas.
4 ozs. green ginger.
2 ozs. ground ginger.
4 ozs. garlic.
¼ oz. cayenne pepper.
1 quart malt vinegar.
Salt to taste.

Cut up apples small, and boil with sugar to the consistency of jam.
Chop up or mince garlic and sultanas.
Add all ingredients to apple and boil for 10 minutes.
Pot and leave for at least 3 months before eating.

282 UNCOOKED CHUTNEY

1 lb. dried apricots.
1¼ pints vinegar.
1½ lbs. onions.
1 lb. stoned dates.
1½ lbs. white sugar.
5 chillies.

Soak apricots and vinegar for a few minutes, then mince all ingredients.
Add sugar, vinegar, and pinch of salt.
Put into pots.
Yield about 6 lbs.

FRUIT AND OTHER DRINKS

283 APPLE ALE

1 gallon cold water.
2 lbs. apples (any kind).
1½ lbs. sugar.
1 oz. root ginger.
½ a level teaspoonful cloves.
½ a level teaspoonful cinnamon.

Wash the apples and grate same, complete with skins, on a suet grater.
Add the pulp to the water, and the cores too, to improve flavour.
Stir the apple water every day for a week and then strain.
Add sugar, ginger (well bruised), cinnamon and cloves, stir until the sugar is dissolved, and leave until the following day.
Then strain through a clean tea-cloth, pour into bottles, cork lightly and leave for a week, when it will be ready for drinking. Makes 1 gallon.

284 BARLEY WINE

1 lb. barley.
1 lb. raisins (cut up).
1 lb. potatoes (grated).
1 orange (sliced).
4 lbs. demerara sugar.
1 gallon boiling water.

Put everything into a bowl and pour on boiling water.
When cool add 1 oz. yeast.
Stir daily for 3 weeks.
Strain well and bottle.

A good wine for colds, taken at bedtime.

285 CHOCOLATE SYRUP

1 cup water.
1 cup sugar.
1 tablespoon butter.
A pinch of salt.
2 tablespoons cocoa.
1 teaspoon vanilla.

Boil together slowly for 5 minutes.
Use 2 tablespoons syrup to 1 glass of milk.
Children love it.

286 CURRANT WINE

3 lbs. currants.
1 gallon cold water.
3 lbs. sugar.

Put fruit and water in a wooden vessel.
Stir daily for 9 days.
Strain off, put in a cask, add 3 lbs. sugar to each gallon.
If you like, add ½ pint brandy to each gallon, when you stop it down 3 days after it has been casked.

287 DAMSON GIN

1 gallon unsweetened gin.
1 gallon damsons, well picked.
2 lbs. caster sugar.

Put all together in a 2-gallon jar or bottle.
Shake well twice a day for 6 weeks.
Strain and bottle, well cork.
Very good.

288 ELDERBERRY SYRUP

Strip ripe berries from stalks, cover with water, simmer for 1 hour, and strain.
Add ½ lb. sugar to each 1 pint juice.
Boil until sugar dissolves.
Bottle.

2 tablespoonsful in a glass filled with hot water is excellent for colds.

289 ELDERFLOWER WINE

1 gallon water.
3 lbs. sugar.
1 quart elder flowers.
1 tablespoon yeast.
1 lb. raisins.
1 pint sherry.
The juice of 1 lemon.
1 egg white.

Boil water and sugar together.
When boiling pour over the flowers and allow to cool.
Add lemon juice and yeast and leave 3 days.
Strain, add egg liquor and wine together, then cook, not too tightly.

290 MIXED FRUIT DRINK

For this you will require:
1 lemon.
1 peach.
½ lb. each of strawberries.
raspberries.
black *or* red currants.

Pulp the fruit well, add the lemon juice, then mix in ½ lb. of icing sugar.
Now pour on 1 quart of boiling water.
Allow to stand, covered, for 12 hours, then strain and serve as required.

291 FRUIT PUNCH

1 cup berries in season *or*
1 cup fruit purée.
1 cup orange juice.
½ cup lemon juice.
1 cup honey.
2 cups cold strong tea.
1 pint ginger ale *or* cider.

Crush berries and mix all ingredients together.
Chill.

292 GRANNY'S GINGER BEER

Boil 1 oz. root ginger in 1 pint water for 10 minutes.
Strain and add 2½ lbs. loaf sugar and 2½ gallons water.
While warm add 1 oz. cream of tartar and ½ oz. tartaric acid and the juice of 1 lemon.
Sprinkle on about ½ oz. yeast.
Leave till next day, then bottle.

293 LEMONADE

8 lemons.
4 lbs. lump sugar.
4 ozs. powdered Epsom salts.
2 ozs. citric acid.
8 breakfastcups boiling water.

Grate rinds and squeeze out juice of lemons, and put with other ingredients.
Pour over boiling water.
Stand, and when cool, bottle.
This essence to be diluted to taste.

294 LEMONADE FOR INVALIDS

1½ pints boiling water.
The juice of 4 lemons.
2 eggs.
The rind of 2 or 3 lemons.
6 ozs. loaf sugar.

Pare off lemon rind very thinly, put it in a jug with the sugar and juice, add water, let it cool, then strain.
Beat the eggs well for 5 minutes in a little of the liquid, then add to the lemon water.

295 MINT TEA

Pour ½ a pint of boiling water on a teaspoon of dried mint, infuse 4 minutes, strain, and add a squeeze of lemon juice and sugar to taste.
Excellent for colds (hot) and refreshing for a cold drink.

296 A CAPITAL NIGHTCAP

Drop 4 drops essence of cloves on 4 lumps loaf sugar, add ½ pint good strong ale and a wineglassful of brandy.
Make it hot and drink before bedtime.

297 RICE AND RAISIN WINE

Boil 6 pints of water and pour on to 1 lb. raisins (large), 1 lb. rice, 3 lbs. white sugar and 1 orange cut up.
Cool to blood heat, then add ½ oz. yeast, spread on toast.
Stir once daily for 21 days.
Strain and bottle.
Ready in 3 months.

298 SLOE WINE

Add 1 pint of boiling water to every pint of sloes.
Let it stand for a week, stirring every day.
Strain and add 1 lb. loaf sugar to every quart of the juice.
Bottle.

299 SYLLABUB

A pint basin of mixed raw and scalded cream.
Nearly ½ a pint of sherry wine.
A little brandy.
The rind and juice of a lemon.
A few almonds, blanched and cut small.
Sugar to your taste.
This quantity fills 18 glasses.

300 TEA WINE

Save 4 pints of cold tea, put into a bowl or jar, add 2 lbs. sugar, ½ lb. large raisins (broken into small pieces), slice 1 orange and 1 lemon, put into liquid.
Stir well and stand for 1 month.
Strain and bottle.
Drinkable in 6 weeks.
Very like sherry.

SALAD DRESSINGS, ETC.

301 BOILED SALAD DRESSING

½ pint milk.
½ teaspoon salt.
1 dessertspoon flour.
¼ pint white vinegar.
2 teaspoons mustard.
2 ozs. sugar.
2 eggs.

Mix dry ingredients together and beat eggs with milk.
Mix all together, then add vinegar *very slowly.*
When mixed put in double saucepan and cook until it thickens, stir frequently.
If liked, more sugar may be added.
Will keep 12 months if bottled.

302 FRENCH DRESSING

This is easy to make and few ingredients are required but they must be of the best quality.
White wine vinegar is essential as ordinary malt vinegar is not fine enough.
Mix salt and pepper to taste in 1 tablespoonful wine vinegar, then add 2 tablespoonfuls olive oil and beat well.
Mustard may also be included as a flavouring, and added with the salt and pepper.

303 MAYONNAISE

1 egg beaten as stiff as possible.
Add ½ pint vegetable oil.
Beat with egg beater all the time the oil is being added.
Just before the last of the oil is added and when it is quite stiff, add 1 teaspoon salt and juice of 1 lemon.
Beat until stiff and add remaining oil.

304 MAYONNAISE

(That will keep)

1 small tin of condensed milk.
Vinegar.
1 egg.
1 teaspoon mustard.
½ teaspoon salt.
½ teaspoon pepper.

Mix mustard to a paste with a little water, add salt and pepper, whisk egg well, add tinned milk, then fill tin with vinegar, and mix into other ingredients. Beat all well together and bottle and use as required.

305 SALAD DRESSING

Mix 1 teaspoon of flour.
1 dessertspoon salt.
½ teaspoon pepper.
4 teaspoons each of dry mustard and salad oil.

When thoroughly mixed, add 4 ozs. sugar.
Beat an egg in a pint of milk, stir in the other ingredients and very gradually add ½ pint vinegar.
Turn into an enamel saucepan and bring to boil until it has thickened, stirring all the time.
When cold, bottle.

MEDICINES

Editor's Note:—As wil be readily understood these items have not all been tried out personally, and I cannot accept responsibility for their effectiveness or otherwise.

Some have been included for their curiosity value.

306 BAKED ONION POULTICE

(Will speedily banish gatherings and boils)

Bake a piece of onion, take out an inner ring and cover the affected part.
Bandage to keep it in place, renew poultice night and morning.
Half an onion can be slowly baked in a tin on top of a gas ring (no need to use the oven).

307 BUTTERCUP OINTMENT

Put ½ lb. pure vaseline into a pan with as many buttercup flowers (without stems) as can possibly be pressed into it.
Allow to simmer (not boil) for ¾ hour.
While still hot, strain through muslin into small pots.
Ready for use when cold.
Very good for all skin troubles.

308 FOR A TICKLING COUGH

Skin some slices of swede.
Put on a plate and sprinkle with brown sugar.
Leave several hours with the plate tilted.
The juice that drains off is soothing and palatable.
Take a teaspoonful when required.

309 ELDERFLOWER FACE CREAM

Melt 1 lb. pure lard in a saucepan and add as many handfuls of elderflowers (stripped from stalks) as the lard will cover.
Simmer gently for about 1 hour.
Strain through a fine sieve or muslin.
Before pouring into small screw top jars, add a few drops of oil of lavender or other good scent.
Use when cold.

310 ELDERFLOWER OINTMENT

1 lb. pure vaseline.
Elder flowers.

Put the vaseline in a saucepan with as many elderflowers (not thick stems) as can possibly be pressed into it. Allow to simmer (not boil) for ½ – ¾ hour.
While very hot, strain through a piece of muslin into small pots.
Ready for use as soon as cold.
Excellent for bruises, sores, insect bites, roughness of skin, etc.

311 FOR RHEUMATISM

Gather dock leaves.
Carefully dry them and bend them around the affected joint.

This cure was given to a friend of mine some years ago by a gypsy. Both my friend and myself have had complete cures by this method.

312 SKIN FOOD

8 ozs. lanolin.
2 ozs. cold cream.
1 oz. castor oil.
½ oz. almond oil.
1 oz. olive oil.
½ teaspoon tincture of benzoin.
1 tablespoon kaolin powder.

Beat the cold cream and lanolin together.
Add oils and kaolin powder, olive oil last.
The longer the cream is beaten the better it will be.

313 SPLINTER IN FINGER

Make a paste of flour and castor oil.
Put the paste around the affected finger or hand and leave for 12 hours, then the splinter will come out easily.

314 WASP STINGS

If you take a piece of tobacco (or break a cigarette into pieces and make it wet) and squeeze the juice on to the sting *immediately,* the pain stops within a matter of seconds and the sting gives no further trouble. Even people allergic to wasp stings respond to this treatment and it is a valuable hint for those with young children. My children all carry half a cigarette each during the wasp season. I have proved it over and over again and everybody to whom I have passed it on has been grateful.

315 TO CURE WHOOPING COUGH

Carry the child afflicted into a sheep-fold and let the sheep breathe on its face, and then lay the child on the spot of ground from which a sheep has just arisen.
Continue this daily for a week.

'Tez a zartin cure, mum I zhuree!'

HANDY HINTS

316 ONIONS

In the wasp season, *always* take an onion to picnics, etc., and have an onion and a knife near the first-aid box.
Onion juice applied *immediately* to a wasp sting stops pain and swelling. If stung in the mouth, chew a bit of raw onion.

317 HOUSEHOLD HINTS

To clean kitchen sink pipe: At night place a large cork in the outlet pipe, then fill sink with hot *soda* water. Next morning remove cork and all grease will come away.

When a hot mark has been accidently made on polished furniture, gently apply a small amount of metal polish on a soft rag and *lightly* rub—the way of the grain. Wipe off and do this again a few times and you will be amazed at the results.

318 SMOOTH RUNNING

Keys will operate more effectively and zip fasteners run more smoothly if properly lubricated.
An excellent non-greasy lubricant is the lead of a pencil.
One treatment will last for months.

319 HERBS, ETC.

Natural iron is contained in spinach, watercress, leeks, raisins, carrots, and lettuce.
Try a bay leaf in a milk pudding.

Use basil in all tomato dishes; good for nervous headaches, in soups.

Lemon sauce should include a pinch of marjoram and a handful of marigold petals in addition to the lemon juice and sugar.

Mint sauce for winter: Mint leaves, allow to stand in a covered vessel with vinegar and brown sugar for three weeks, then strain and boil the liquid.

Mint tea: Good for indigestion; make as ordinary tea.

Parsley tea: Good for rheumatism. One tablespoon to a pint of boiling water; or, cover and leave to get cold, strain, and take freely an hour before each meal.

Sage tea: Good for sore throats and colds, though too much may cause indigestion. Sage is said to keep ants away.

320 FOR CLEANING FURNITURE

½ pint methylated.
½ pint linseed oil.
½ pint malt vinegar.

Mix, and let mature for a few weeks, and shake it often to get it mixed.

321 TO CLEAN FURNITURE

Clean *Mahogany* with equal parts of vinegar and water.
Walnut with a piece of flannel dipped in paraffin.
Ebony with a soft rag dipped in olive oil.
Limed Oak with a soft rag dipped in dry metal polish.
Oak furniture with warm beer.

For *Blue Bloom* on furniture, use a pad dampened with vinegar and warm water. Follow up with an application of good furniture cream, and then polish with a soft chamois duster.

322 FRENCH POLISH

¼ lb. white wax.
1 oz. beeswax.
½ oz. castile soap.
½ pint turpentine.
¼ pint boiling water.

Dissolve the wax in the turpentine and the soap in the water, and mix all together.

323 FURNITURE OIL

½ pint linseed oil.
¼ pint turpentine.
¼ pint methylated.
¼ pint vinegar.

INDEX

DEVON SPECIALS

SOUPS

FISH DISHES

MEAT DISHES

SAVOURY SNACKS AND SUPPER DISHES

PUDDINGS AND SWEETS

105 Banana Surprise
106 Blackberry Charlotte
107 Chocolate Pudding
108 Coffee Fridge Cake
109 Cheesecake (Baked)
110 Cleopatra Puddings
111 Date, Apple and Cornflake Pudding
112 Dutch Apple Cake Pudding
113 German Apple Tart
114 Glamour Sweet Dish
115 Ginger Meringue
116 One of Grandma's Sweets
117 Hazelnut Meringue Gateau
118 Hazelnut Flan
119 Iced Currants
120 Konfit Shortbread
121 Lemon Fluff
122 Lemon Meringues
123 Lemon Pudding
124 Lemon Crunch
125 Lemon Tart
126 Marzipan Mixture
127 Minature Rice Puddings
128 Traditional Rice Pudding
129 Mock Mousse
130 New Plum Tart
131 Pineapple Whip
132 Pavlova
133 Princess Pudding
134 Sago Plum Pudding
135 To Cook Rhubarb
136 Swiss Cream
137 Strawberry Layer Gateau
138 Teacup Pudding
139 Treacle George
140 Pineapple Upside-Down Pudding
141 Toby's Chocolate Pudding
142 Velvet Cream
143 Walnut Cream Flan
144 Steamed Syrup Sponge

CAKES AND BISCUITS

SCONES AND BREAD, ETC.

CHRISTMAS RECIPES

VEGETARIAN RECIPES

MICROWAVE RECIPES

JAMS, ETC.

CHUTNEYS AND PICKLES

FRUIT AND OTHER DRINKS

SALAD DRESSINGS, ETC.

MEDICINES

HANDY HINTS

320 For Cleaning Furniture
321 To Clean Furniture
322 French Polish
323 Furniture Oil